THE POWER OF
SILENCE

THE POWER OF SILENCE

SILENCE

The Riches That Lie Within

GRAHAM TURNER

B L O O M S B U R Y

NEW YORK • LONDON • NEW DELHI • SYDNEY

Published by Bloomsbury USA, New York

All papers used by Bloomsbury USA are natural, recyclable products made from
wood grown in well-managed forests. The manufacturing processes conform to
the environmental regulations of the country of origin.

LIBRARY OF CONGRESS CATALOGING-IN-PUBLICATION DATA HAS BEEN APPLIED FOR.

ISBN: 978-1-62040-102-6

First U.S. Edition 2013

1 3 5 7 9 10 8 6 4 2

Typeset by Fakenham Prepress Solutions, Fakenham, Norfolk NR21 8NN, U.K.
Printed in the U.S.A.

To Jim, who first corralled me into silence

CONTENTS

PREFACE

This book is an account of a journey through the world of those who value silence, and I began it expecting I knew not what. Certainly not the richness and variety which I was led to discover. I say 'led' because that world inexorably drew me in, as if the process had a will of its own quite apart from my own wishes.

Tapping rather uncertainly on all kinds of doors, trying to find my bearings, to grope my way towards some understanding of what, in truth, seemed like a rather nebulous subject, I constantly found new worlds, new perspectives opening up before me.

It was the first time in a long experience of writing that I had had the feeling of a subject taking me over, having its way with me.

At the beginning, I never suspected just how rich, important and fulfilling silence can be, how universal its usefulness. In places which most of us initially associate with noise – the concert hall and the theatre – I found musicians and actors only too ready to talk about its value.

In India, which bids fair to be the world's noisiest country, I found a civilisation which still, amidst all the racket, reveres silence as the very heart of spiritual life.

In America, I found a university which is based on the practise of meditation.

In the Lebanon, I found a group of people who trust to what they find in meditative silence to try to give their fragile country the help it so often needs.

What a marvellous, if often gruelling, adventure writing this book turned out to be! It gave me a chance to look at life through the eyes of hermits in the Egyptian desert; to meet an American Zen master in Paris, of all places; to explore the ways in which psychotherapists use silence to try to ease the agonies of the human psyche; and to hear a self-confessed murderer in a Scottish prison speak of what he has found through silent meditation.

Encounter after encounter revealed the priceless gifts which silence yields to an extraordinary array of people. It left me feeling that it is the most under-used and under-valued of all our personal resources. You only have to see the quality of the lives of those who devote themselves to it to realise its immense potential.

It is difficult to acknowledge, by name, all the people who so generously gave their time to talk to me about what silence means to them. Suffice it to say that I am grateful to every one of them.

I am, though, particularly grateful to the Anglican Bishop of London, the Rt Rev Richard Chartres, without whose aid I would not have been so warmly welcomed in the desert monasteries of Egypt; to Michael Billington, theatre critic of the Guardian, who gave his time unstintingly and introduced me to Penelope Wilton; to Richard Johnson, who arranged my journeys around the world of TM; and to my friend Peter Riddell who – with the aid of modern technology which I lack – managed a steady stream of email traffic, turned up useful facts and arranged all my journeys with seemingly inexhaustible patience.

And, finally, to my wife Jean, whose encouragement and editorial skills were much in demand and to whom this book owes a great deal.

1

Silence? No thanks!

For many people in the West, the very idea of silence is strange and unattractive, if not actually forbidding. You only have to think of the way we commonly describe it to realise that it is not something most of us look forward to. We talk about an uncomfortable silence, an awkward silence, an embarrassing silence, an oppressive silence, a stony silence, an ominous silence, a silence you can cut with a knife, a deathly silence.

That doesn't include all those people who regard the absence of talk and noise and the activity which usually goes with them as downright boring, a waste of precious time when you might be *doing* something interesting or listening to something entertaining.

'Our culture in the United States', said an office manager in Albuquerque, New Mexico, 'is extremely good at bombarding us with words and images, so silence has become counter-cultural in this country. The children I know don't even have a concept of silence any longer, except as a notion of emptiness, a scary void. They no longer know how to be quiet and I'm afraid that's true for Americans as a whole'.

'Silence doesn't have much of a take in this country', agreed one of her friends. 'It's thought of as something appropriate to a time of sorrow and people would say "I don't want to sign up for sorrow today."'

As for giving time to silent contemplation, that – apart from anything else – might cost money. 'This is a very dynamic, gregarious society', said a neuroscientist in Iowa who practises Transcendental Meditation. 'It wants to build and create, so you shouldn't sit there with your eyes closed, but get the bricks and mortar out! If you happen to be a lawyer and you close your eyes for a couple of minutes, that's billable, that's 50 dollars.'

So, for many people, in the Western world at least, there is no longer anything appealing about the prospect of being quiet. How many of us ever talk about a delightful or enjoyable silence? It is thought of as an impediment to social ease, a potentially malign zone. The idea that conversation at a dinner party might suddenly dry up fills the average host and hostess with dread.

Silence, in fact, is widely regarded as nothing more than a disagreeable hole that must be filled at all costs and by whatever means come to hand. Every combine-harvester driver worth his salt has a stereo system in his cab. Joggers – even of the green persuasion – are unlikely to issue forth without their earphones. Hundreds of millions engage in a global talk-fest by text and mobile. We twitter and tweet endlessly. And more and more of us turn up the decibels to banish the tedium and emptiness of life with consoling or exhilarating sound. Noise has become our default setting, silence an ever more alien concept.

Partly out of tradition, it is also considered to have some connection with religion and, for a good many people, that is yet another reason to steer well clear of it. Even churchgoers do not always know what to do with it. Asked by a friend who seldom darkens the door of a church what he ought to do when the minister called for a moment's silence, one faithful member of the flock replied: 'Oh, I just bow my head, count to 20 and then sit up again.' Phew! Thank goodness that's over, then!

Those in the Western world who go away on religious retreats are apt to be regarded as dangerously introspective navel-gazers. To most, it is as eccentric a pursuit as bungee jumping. Even churchgoers suspect that there is something just a little unhealthy about wanting *that* much quiet.

I asked a couple of female friends what they thought about silence and both confessed that they did not like the idea at all, because it made them feel uneasy if not downright apprehensive. 'To me,' said a farmer's wife, 'silence is eerie, deathly – and black. If there's something happening, I'm fine, but, when things go quiet, I get nervous.' A second woman, a retired teacher, also wanted none of it. 'It means,' she said, 'that you might suddenly start thinking, and most people are afraid of what they might think.'

In her mind, in other words, there is no protection in silence. In those potentially blank, wide-open spaces of the mind, you have no defence against the fears and anxieties which most of us are prey to – relationships which are not going well, unhappy memories we would rather suppress, things we know we should do something about but have not, ailments we would rather forget about. A protracted silence, we sense, could open up that agenda of anxieties that we prefer to keep at bay with activity and noise. Ironically, silence has come to be regarded, in the West at least, as almost the antithesis of peace of mind.

'Silence', said Father Richard Rohr, an American Franciscan priest whose books have sold more than a million copies, 'would make people in this country feel meaningless. Here, you make yourself significant by saying smart things, making clever put-downs, using words to fill up the moment. To Americans, silence feels like an entrance into emptiness. And on the psychological level, there's also a fear of facing yourself, a fear of the self-knowledge which is invariably incriminating.'

That hardly sounds like an inviting prospect, and there is certainly nothing intrinsically benign about silence. It can deepen the loneliness of the already lonely. It is the arena where we struggle with our regrets, our yearnings and our resentments, which all too often are unresolved and unhealed. Human beings, moreover, can use it in the most merciless and callous of ways. It is apt to be a weapon of choice in once-loving relationships that have turned sour. It can be deployed to freeze people out, to cut them off from the oxygen of social inter-course. Things that should never have been spoken can leave, in the ensuing silence, a terrible legacy of bitterness. Things that *ought* to have been spoken but never were can blight whole lives.

Then there are the silences we impose upon ourselves because our memories are too painful for words. Such is the silence of tens of millions who have endured the horrors of war. Such is the silence of many of those who survived the Holocaust. Such was the silence of Tomas Reichental from Slovakia who was sent to the Bergen-Belsen concentration camp when he was only nine years old.

'I was silent about it for 55 years', he said. 'After I married I never told my wife or my children about the camp. We lived in freezing conditions there, I was starving, there were thousands of bodies lying around, the stench was indescribable, and I just couldn't bear to speak about it. Whenever there was a TV programme about those things, I used to switch it off. It felt like a heavy burden inside me for all those years. It was terribly painful. It was always there but I tried to bypass it.'

'I only began to speak of it when a teacher at my grandchild's school here in Dublin asked if I would talk to the children about those unspeakable horrors, that living death. The first time I spoke, I broke down in tears, and so did the teacher.'

Thus too Annette, who lives in the English Midlands and who lost many of her family in the Holocaust and still, to this day, has nightmares about it. She does not speak about it even to her husband. Best to try to forget, she thinks, but she still carries a terrible silence within.

So is there anything either positive or useful about silence? Or is it nothing more than either a mental attic where terrible memories have been stowed away or else a series of damnable longueurs that have to be negotiated by any of the means available to us?

Some religious folk, though by no means all, venerate silence as the space in which we can hear the voice of conscience (or even God), transcend the ego, rediscover our better selves, reconnect with 'the essence of our being' (in the case of Hindus) or attain a state of enlightenment (in the case of Buddhists). That is hardly surprising. They have traditions to be honoured, creeds to propound. But what about the irreligious multitude, who may recognise and practise virtue better than some 'believers' but yet want nothing to do with doctrines which seem to them either irrational or downright bizarre. What, one might think, can silence possibly hold for them?

Yet, as I have discovered, it is not only the religious who regard silence as precious. Without what it brings forth from their patients, psychotherapists would find their job infinitely more difficult, if not impossible. Actors insist that playing the silences in a drama is just as important as speaking the words; musicians that the pauses are as vital as the notes; while, as Sir Neil MacGregor, director of the British Museum, points out, silence is 'an absolute *sine qua non*' in the appreciation of art.

It is also valued, even revered, by some rather more surprising people. 'In the big mountains,' said Stephen Venables, the first Briton to reach the summit of Everest alone and without the aid of oxygen, 'noise equates to danger. The ice under your feet can go off like a pistol shot in the middle of the night, there's the terrifying roar of cliffs collapsing, rock faces falling apart, snow avalanches, huge masses succumbing to changes in temperature and gravity – and you certainly don't want to be in their way.'

'By contrast, silence means that everything is still and safe. So I love silence. It's what I want. And it has never intensified anxiety in me when I was alone.'

'When I got to the summit of Everest that day in 1988, it was late afternoon and just starting to snow, but the wind hadn't got up so there was a sort of blanketing effect and that silence had the most powerful quality. I was potentially in a very dangerous place, utterly alone with five or six billion people down below, and yet I was in that calm, serene silence. It felt almost like a blessing.'

For Ian Player (brother of the golfer Gary), who over the course of many years has taken thousands of people on trails into the South African wilderness, silence was a necessity as well as a blessing.

All the walking, he said, had to be done in complete silence, because some animals can hear the sound of a human voice as much as two miles away. It was also an essential safety precaution because 'the different calls of birds will tell you if there are buffaloes or hippos around, so you have to have your ears about you'.

The rigours of the trail, he went on, were always a challenge, but 'without doubt, by far the most difficult job I had to do was ensure that people kept quiet while we were trekking. It often took me three days to get them to shut up and listen. For the first couple of days they hated it, in fact they could hardly stand it. Not surprising really, because they had come from a world which is drowning in noise.

'People now are just afraid of any kind of silence and I had to keep on telling them to shut up – and in no uncertain terms, because they would just go on talking. The worst were the Americans and the Germans.

'Yet, you know, in the end the silence had a profound effect on many of those people. After all, if you go to a place like the Umfolozi Reserve, you're going back 250,000 years, to a primal part of yourself when nobody had cellphones or watches or computers – and, by the end of the trek, the people who came with me had a little taste of that primal world. When they left many of them would weep, the men as well as the women.'

I had just a taste of the same primal world in the Swiss Alps, the Rockies and the Egyptian deserts, places where a profound silence is still in command. In this book I want to explore the world of those who regard silence as a valuable companion, a source of inspiration, who find in it not an emptiness but a plenitude, a richness which those who shun it are missing.

What exactly does it mean to actors, musicians and psychotherapists? Does it have a use even for those who are condemned to spend many years of their lives behind prison bars? And what of those who turn to it as a way of transforming their lives, who regard it, as one Christian put it, as 'a meeting place where I am looking for God's love and He is looking for mine'. Such ardour suggests that it could be a good deal more than a blank and boring space.

It is very easy to see why so many people run away from silence, but it is, after all, our own little world, the mental space we carry around with us all the time, and it does seem rather odd that we should care so little about it and its potential value – as little, in fact, as most of us cared about our planet even 50 years ago. Might it not be worth considering what our own private planet has to offer us? At the moment, for most of us in the West, it is just one of the great unknowns.

Not so in the East. There, a very different philosophy prevails. 'Silence', said a dentist friend from Bangalore in India, 'is very much part of our culture.' I cannot conceive of anyone in the West making such a statement. It does seem to come from another planet.

Why do Indians, why does the East, have such a different mind-set, a mind-set which reverences silence instead of shrinking back from it? What do the Indians see in silence that most of us plainly don't?

2

India: Silence in the genes

There may be noisier countries than India, but I cannot think of one offhand. Every truck carries the invitation 'Horn OK Please', and journeys in cities such as Mumbai can feel like one continuous beep. London is a morgue by comparison.

The horn, in fact, is one of the principal languages of India. One beep means 'I'm coming past', two 'I'm coming whether you like it or not', three 'don't do that on any account'.

Indians themselves are equally voluble. 'We talk maximum and maximum volume too', as one of my Indian friends put it. Conversations between groups of men can sound like the rattle of competing machine guns. Even Hindu temples are places of bells and chants and chattering rather than silence.

Yet, despite the constant racket – or perhaps even because of it – there is a deep respect for the spiritual value of silence among Muslims as well as Hindus, Buddhists and Jains. 'It is the most respected part of our culture', said my dentist friend, Ravi Rao, who is Hindu. 'It's not as important as it was in Gandhiji's time, but there are still many people who take time to be silent.'

'They will let you know that they are on *maun vrat*, which means that they've taken a vow to be silent for a day, a week or even a year. You hear of people who haven't said anything for years. The practise of silence is still widely revered and it's still regarded as a road to wisdom.'

'After all, it's in silence that we reflect on the truths we have come across in life. Everything is born in silence – all thoughts, all wisdom, all perspective. Without it, you'll never see things as they really are, you'll always be ruled by your reactions – and, as those reactions prey on your mind and increase in intensity, it'll ruin your peace.'

The respect for silence is rooted in traditions that go back thousands of years. 'Silence and its value are in the Indian gene', said Jaya Row, who teaches Vedanta, one of the philosophical schools of Hinduism. 'It's the way we're brought up and it's still the culture even though things have deteriorated since Gandhi died. There is a great and hidden respect for silence.'

India is not merely the home of ten million gurus (meaning, literally, someone who dispels darkness) and bogus gurus, with, all too often, a talent for purveying the weirdest of religious notions. It also offers an apparently endless range of techniques for achieving spiritual enlightenment, all of which seem to involve the practise of silence.

It is at the very heart of yoga, aside from curry the best-known of India's exports. There are, of course, physical aspects to yoga, but to the cognoscenti they are always subordinate to the silent and meditative ones.

'I'd call the more popular forms of yoga a kind of preliminary yoga', said Dr Shrikrishna, who has been teaching it for over 30 years. 'If I have a pain in my back, I naturally want to cure it. But the idea that yoga only involves moving your limbs and stretching your body is nonsense. That is only the start.'

'The main point of yoga is to silence all the inner noise which prevents us from experiencing what is beyond, so that we can discover what it is that makes us feel disquiet and a lack of peace. Then, in that same silence, to deal with the things which are creating that disquiet – not to try to escape from them, but to confront them.'

In the West, he said, the vast majority never went beyond the starting-point. For them, yoga was a fashionable, efficient way of keeping in good shape but with very little, if any, of its deeper challenge; servicing the body but not giving the soul a look-in.

'In America,' Shrikrishna went on, 'yoga's more superficial forms have become part of the mainstream. Ten per cent of the country is said to be involved with it in some form. You can even go on yoga holidays. Very few go to the deeper levels.'

In Europe, he said, there were psycho-therapeutic approaches which also did not require you to look at yourself too keenly. Indian spiritual development through yoga, by contrast, meant that 'nothing is allowed to remain hidden, there is no sweeping of things under the carpet. It is real carpet-cleaning, and, if I'm the one who is beating the carpet, the dust is going to rise.'

'When you engage with yourself in real silence, you can find two things. First, how to deal with the events and situations in life which create noise and disquiet in you, and, second, you can find out who you really are. That is real spiritual development. You have to let everything come up and deal with it. Being able to harmonise all the situations which arise in life is the fruit of deep inner silence.'

'Sometimes the Western approach is "don't disturb yourself, you're disturbed enough already!" My goal is not to make you happy, but to disturb you so that you start to challenge your current wisdom.' He spends a good part of his year 'carpet-cleaning' in seminars throughout Europe.

There is also nothing superficial or half-hearted about the Buddhist technique known as vipassana, often called insight meditation, which the Dalai Lama practises regularly. Rhea D'Souza, a young Protestant Christian who with a partner runs a consultancy business in Mumbai, had just come back from a ten-day vipassana course when I met her.

The silent meditation, she said, had started at 3.30 in the morning and ended at 9.30 in the evening. There were short breaks and the usual mealtimes. The food was good but simple and there were no distractions – 'no reading, no music, not even so much as looking at each other.' She had been one of 200 women of all ages and there were long waiting-lists, because demand for the courses was so high. One Chinese girl she had met was doing the course for the fourth time.

She herself had signed up for it, said Rhea, because she was aware that she talked and laughed a lot, and had wondered if she had allowed herself to become stereotyped as a certain kind of person. 'I asked myself whether I was laughing and talking so much because I wanted to or because I was just trying to live up to the stereotype and couldn't remain silent. The only way to find out was to experiment.'

At first, she'd had difficulty during the times of meditation in keeping her mind from wandering and her body still, sitting as she was in the half-lotus position – 'I kept fidgeting and shifting around' – but by the second day she had begun to settle down and enjoy herself.

'As the time went by', she recalled, 'the joy in me was amazing, I found myself smiling inside. I was never bored. During the three-hour meditation every afternoon, a gong would ring at the end of each hour to give us a chance to take a five-minute break, but I just didn't want one. It was like being in a beautiful garden, I just wanted to go on sitting there.'

After the course had finished, Rhea went on, people were given permission to talk to each other 'to ease us back into the world of noise. I was interested that the 200 men who'd been on a parallel course started chattering immediately, whereas the women were much slower to start speaking. I didn't want to say anything.

'I came away from the course very happy to have found that there *is* another me who can be totally silent. And that other me was one I'd discovered rather than one I'd created.' A new self to enrich and complement the old, in fact. There was more to silence than Rhea had imagined.

The course, she added, had helped her enormously in other ways. It had somehow given her a new strength. The marriage of one of her female relatives had subsequently broken down, she had attempted suicide by taking pills and had been desperately sick in hospital for a long time. 'As I'd grown up', said Rhea, 'I could never stand hospitals – I used to try to hold my breath while I was there – but, this time, I was actually able to stay in hospital to be near her. Silence has grown in me, so that now I can be completely quiet inside even when I'm doing something. That healing silence is a living reality for me because that's where I get my strength.'

And what of India's tens of millions of Muslims? What is Islam's take on silence? I had been trying for months to get in touch by telephone with one of India's leading Islamic scholars, Maulana Wahiduddin Khan – but had failed dismally.

So, in Delhi and with time to spare, I decided that there was nothing to be lost in at least going to look for him in the suburb of Nizamuddin, not knowing whether he would be at home even if I could find the place.

The ride there, by motorised rickshaw, was both terrifying and exhilarating. All I had to go on was the address of the local Islamic Centre, which turned out to be a rather dusty accumulation of books in a well-worn building at the far end of an arcade.

There seemed no point in being diffident, so I declared boldly that I had come to see the Maulana as if a meeting had already been arranged. The elder of the two men there, clearly somewhat taken aback, instructed his junior to lead me to the Maulana's home. We walked through muddy lanes until we came to a substantial white house that had both a guard and a high metal fence.

I said again that I had come to see the Maulana and, after a muttered conversation between the guard and my guide, I was ushered into a lower chamber. It seemed that the Maulana was at least at home. After a long and somewhat uncomfortable silence, I was told that he had, in fact, agreed to see me if I would come back in the afternoon.

Again with time to spare, I decided to set off on foot through the slums of Nizamuddin, its narrow alleys teeming with goats and motor bikes, to see if I could find an organisation, also unreachable by telephone, which was said to be run by people who followed the tradition of the Sufis, Muslim mystics who seek to achieve union with God through silent contemplation.

Again, all I had to go on was the organisation's mysterious-sounding name – Dargah Hazrat Inayat Khan – and an address in English, not much use in a place where nobody seemed to speak the language. By multiple inquiries and some sort of miracle, I none the less found my way to its modest headquarters and to its executive director, Samiur Rahman.

He told me that, following the Sufi tradition, the trust aimed to serve the poorest of the poor. They offered free music and handicraft teaching and gave a cup of milk each day to everyone who came to their door. He also had no doubt as to the value of silence.

'It is quite simply the realm where God exists,' he said, 'and it is the silence which helps you make a connection with Allah. When you visit a place of beauty, the forests or the seashore, and when you think of that beauty, you are immediately connected to Him. That is the nature of silence. How do you internalise that feeling? You internalise it in silence!'

It was the same when a Muslim went on the *haj*, the pilgrimage to Mecca. 'At every point', he went on, 'you feel that Allah is speaking to you in the silence. It isn't a voice, just a strong feeling. As you mingle with the crowds, you feel that He is there with you.'

And so to the Maulana, who turned out to be a distinguished-looking old man with a straggly white beard, dressed in a long, mud-brown cloak. With his daughter and grand-daughter as aides, he immediately embarked on an account of what silence means to Muslims.

In Islamic thought, he said, there were two kinds of silence. The first, meditation, was – so to speak – heart-based and sought to tap the insights and instincts that we all kept hidden there. Only those Muslims who followed the Sufi philosophy believed in it.

The second, or contemplation, was essentially mind-based. That was the sort of silence he himself tried to practise, and it was the kind of silence which the main body of Muslim scholars, the *ulema*, also favoured. If you read the Koran, the Maulana went on, you would find that there were almost 500 verses that told us we have to ponder everything in the world, including ourselves. Through that sort of contemplation, you could discover the truth about both the world and yourself.

To indicate that he was not just offering a personal opinion, the Maulana quoted a series of the Prophet Mohammed's own sayings, or *hadiths*, of which he said there were six collections. In one, it was recorded that the Prophet told his followers 'You have to keep silence', in another that he had said 'One who keeps silence will be rewarded with salvation.' In Islam, added the Maulana, silence was 'a rewardable act' and the reward was Paradise, which meant living in the neighbourhood of God.

Silence had a place in all the basic Islamic practises, he went on. In the five daily times of worship, for example, there were prayers which were recited out loud, others which you said to yourself, in the silence of your heart. It was in *that* silence that you could establish contact with Almighty God.

As for the month of Ramadan, that was a time when the Prophet himself had always gone into both silence and seclusion, either for ten days or, sometimes, for the whole month. That process of seeking seclusion was called *aytakkuf* in Arabic and it involved thinking about both the world and yourself in silence.

Most of today's Muslims, said the Maulana, knew only the *forms* of Islam and not its deeper spirit. They might go to a mosque during Ramadan and sit in silence, but that was merely the form of *aytakkuf*. The spirit was to keep silent and contemplate. The real point of Ramadan was not merely to avoid eating and drinking during certain hours, but to go into silence and keep yourself free from all forms of distraction.

As to whether God actually spoke to people in some kind of voice or simply by inspiration through our thoughts, the Maulana said that, according to Islamic belief, God communicated with human beings in two ways. One was by revelation and then God actually spoke in words. That, however, was quite exceptional: He had only done it once and that was to the Prophet. For all other Muslims, the communication came not verbally but by inspiration. In both cases, the messengers were thought to be angels – spiritual, unseen beings.

So silence for Muslims was not merely saying nothing, it meant seeking in quiet for the deeper meaning of life. 'It is', said the Maulana, 'like travelling beyond space and time, trying to establish contact with a higher reality.' As it seemed to him, silence was really a higher form of speaking, speaking without actually using words.

The whole of Islam, in fact, was based on silence. He would like, he said, to tell me a story. The Prophet had been with some of his companions and they had shared a happy experience. Afterwards his companions had said in very loud voices 'Allahu Akbar' (God is great). 'God', the Prophet had rebuked them, 'is not deaf!' Of course, added the Maulana wryly, 'those who speak on public platforms, our political leaders, have no time for that sort of contemplation. They want nothing to do with silence.'

No one I talked to in India seemed to have a bad word to say about silence. They might not practise it, they might lead the noisiest of lives, but no one spoke of being worried about silence, still less afraid of it. The very idea would, indeed, have struck them as bizarre. Everyone I talked to spoke of silence with a certain respect and, in many cases, reverence.

As the days went by, I could not help wondering why there should be such a gulf between our two worlds. After all, for many centuries Christianity also had a strong contemplative tradition. Silence was at the heart of monastic life and, during the Middle Ages, it was generally regarded as a vital part of Christian practise. Lent, like Ramadan, was originally meant to be a time of silent contemplation as well as self-denial: less chatter as well as less self-indulgence.

Nobody puts the widely accepted Christian view of silence better than the seventh-century bishop and theologian, Isaac of Nineveh. 'Many', he wrote, 'are avidly seeking, but they alone find who remain in continual silence. Every man who delights in a multitude of words, even though he says admirable things, is empty within. If you love truth, be a lover of silence. Silence, like the sunlight, will illuminate you in God and deliver you from the phantoms of ignorance.'

Thousands of others in monasteries across the Christian world at that time would have echoed his words. Yet, for whatever reason, that Christian tradition has atrophied to the point where it is now the preserve of a tiny minority of believers. Richard Chartres, the Anglican Bishop of London, believes that this is partly because we in the West have spent the last 250 years mapping the outer world – an exercise which gave us extraordinary global power – but, in the process, we have forgotten that 'there is a truth to be harvested within ourselves'. 'We've got to the point', he said, 'where we have become incapable of seeing the *inner* truth of anything.'

Laurence Freeman, a Benedictine monk who runs an organisation which is trying to revive that contemplative tradition, entirely agrees. 'Yes,' he said, 'we've spent centuries mapping the outer world and thinking about God, but we don't take a break to actually *be* with Him, and that is why going to church is often so exhaustively boring.

'We need a far more balanced spiritual diet in the West, because in the Western church we have gorged ourselves on the carbohydrates of words and the greasy, fatty foods of dogmas and doctrines.' As I was to discover, silence is still greatly valued in the worlds of theatre and music and in the practise of psychotherapy, but in our churches it is often drowned out in an almost ceaseless torrent of words and music.

In India, by contrast, the tradition of silence has never lost its lustre. The ancient Hindu scriptures which are at its root –the Upanishads (which means sitting at the feet of the guru) and the Vedas – were written centuries before the birth of Christ and are the outcome of the solitude and silence of a multitude of rishis, or wise men.

'Much of the wisdom was written down in our great books, the Vedas, the original scriptures', said Ravi Rao. 'There are four of them and they came from silence. They were not written by one person. Their authors, the rishis, went away into the mountains, forests and caves and meditated in silence, thinking about life and their experience and the basic questions of "who am I?" and "where did the world come from?'

'It was all a process of thinking, it wasn't based on anything said dogmatically. It wasn't born out of anyone's preaching. The Vedas and the Upanishads are the product of minds searching for the truth.'

'The rishis', agreed Rajmohan Gandhi, grandson of the Mahatma, 'discovered their truths in silence, but it was a silence mingled with curiosity about the nature of truth, the nature of life, the nature of the world, and different rishis came to different conclusions.

'All that accumulated reflection and contemplation has not produced a unified body of doctrine. The Vedas and Upanishads offer alternative explanations for these huge questions. Yes, it's à la carte and not table d'hôte. The Indian spiritual tradition is full of passionate and, at times, violent debate, and what has come down to us is a variety of explanations to pick and choose from!'

The Vedas were very different from the Christian and Islamic holy books, said Om Prakash, an Indian businessman. 'They weren't spoken by a messenger, like Jesus or Mohammed, and the truths which our seers offered us weren't issued as commandments. They weren't a sermon like the Sermon on the Mount and they didn't say "you must do this but not that." They simply presented the truths they had seen.'

The same spirit is evident in the Bhagavadgita, the most famous of the Hindu sacred texts, written about 200 years before the birth of Christ. 'There are no do's and don'ts in the Gita', remarked a Hindu nun whom I met. 'There are always three opinions – good, better and best and bad, worse and worst – and you have to choose. It's very different from the Koran and the Bible.

'After the discourse between the god-like Krishna and the warrior-prince Arjuna, Krishna tells Arjuna "I've explained the knowledge to you, now you'd better make up your own mind. If you can't make a decision, ask somebody who knows better and then, if you must, come back to me'. Just as in the Vedas, all 10,000 verses of them, there are no commandments.'

Many Hindus, the nun went on, were linked to their traditions in another way. 'We are taught', she said, 'that our forefathers were rishis and that each family descendant is connected to a particular rishi. When someone asks "what is your *gotra*?" it means "which rishi are you connected to and of which rishis are you a descendant?" It is perhaps not wholly dissimilar to the idea of patron saints.

The practise of silence can prove a salvation for devout Hindus like the businessman Om Prakash. When I met him, he had just come back from a few days at an ashram in a remote village in the Himalayas.

'I am a Westernised man', he said. 'I studied at an American Jesuit college. That strongly shaped my life. When I came home, I discovered that my uncle, who founded the tea machinery business in India, had deified industriousness. He'd put up slogans around the factory such as "Work is Worship'.

'That, too, took me away from the essence of my being, and I became a programmable, usable person. My failing has always been hyperactivity, speed and noise. That wasn't just the effect of the business, it's part of my nature.

'My restlessness scarred me and created problems for others, but the company wanted the fruits of my restlessness. It was all head and my uncle discouraged anything to do with the heart because it wasn't thought useful.'

The idea of putting a premium on the mind as opposed to the heart, he added, was a Western concept, and 'it became superimposed on our culture because it produced material so-called goodies.

We were mesmerised by it.' (And still are, I felt like adding, having seen what goes on in cities such as Mumbai.)

Then, almost 40 years ago, he came across the idea of silent meditation, which soon yielded a very different sort of fruit. 'We were in the throes of an eight-and-a-half-year conflict with our workers. Then my uncle had a heart attack and I was praying for his recovery when the thought suddenly came to me "have you ever prayed for that fitter who you know has been ill for six months?"'

'I'd come to believe that there is a magic in unfettered obedience to intuitions of that kind, so I left the prayer hall, went straight to the fitter's home, begged his pardon, told him that he must get treatment – and offered to pay for it myself.'

'The news of that spread like wildfire in the factory. I had allowed my heart to take over from my head for the first time. The fitter said nothing to me, but it led to the end of the dispute. I invited the union leader and his colleagues to come to my home for a cup of tea. Previously I'd been scared of him.'

'They had no fewer than 32 demands, so I asked them to list the ones which they felt were really legitimate and promised that I would fight to get them accepted. The dispute was sorted out within days.'

Silence, Om Prakash went on, had not come easily to him. It was the antithesis of all he had been used to. 'In the old days, I used to get so charged up that I had to get away for a rest. But the rishis saw long ago that we can only come face to face with our nature, and try to deal with it, in silence. How else?'

'Practising silence every day, as I do now, doesn't mean that I've become a cabbage. It does mean that I try to turn away from all kinds of compulsive activity, physical and mental, one thought on the coat-tails of another.'

To that end, he spends an hour and a half every day, morning and evening, in complete silence. He begins with 38 exercises that tense and relax the various parts of his body. That, he says, prepares him for meditation. Then he tries to still his mind by watching his breath go in and out. Finally, he uses an ancient yoga technique that comes from the Veda and has been passed down from guru to guru. He then sits in silence. 'If I didn't do that', he said, 'it would be like cooking a meal and then not eating it!'

'My prayer each day before I begin is "Heavenly Father, Divine Mother, Friend, Beloved God, Jesus Christ and the saints and seers of all the ages, I bow to you all. Lead me from ignorance to wisdom, from restlessness to peace, from desire to contentment.'

'Then I ask that I will be granted the precious boons of health, vitality and deep inner silence, so that I may experience bliss and share it with others. Yes, I do expect God to speak to me, but that comes in the form of intuitions. They come not from the outside, but from the best of us inside. Silence nurtures that side of you.'

He listed the fruits of silence as he had experienced it. A silent body, he said, 'is like a well-kept home – clean, uncluttered and airy.' A silent mind is 'free of me and mine, of likes and dislikes, of hates and hurts, of attractions and aversions.' A silent heart is 'full of love, gratitude, generosity, forgiveness and compassion.' A silent intellect is 'free of dogmas, fixations and isms.'

'These four things', he said, 'take you to the temple of silence and that is what I have experienced. You can call that temple the Kingdom of God, if you like, a place where everything will be added unto you.

If those four things are not the Kingdom of God, I'd like to know what is!'

In all my travels for this book, I met no more fervent, convinced (and convincing) advocate of the virtues of silence than Om Prakash. It is hard to quibble with his ardour, and the price he pays in terms of daily discipline. He seems to be a happy, peaceful and fulfilled human being. He is certainly a most unusual businessman.

He is also living proof of the fact that what the rishis passed down has not been entirely lost. His story is a perfect illustration of the pick-and-mix nature of Hinduism.

Meeting the Maulana and the Sufi-inspired benefactors of Nizamuddin had whetted my appetite to find out more about Sufis, these Muslim mystics who believe that God is within us and that the best way to get in touch with Him is in silence. At that stage, it had not even occurred to me that it might be possible to meet a living Sufi.

I called on Wajahat Habibullah, a scion of one of India's most distinguished Muslim families and formerly the country's Information Commissioner. A cultured and profoundly spiritual man, he lives in a comfortable villa on the Lodi Estate, where many of the great and good of Delhi have their homes. He is plainly no Anglophobe. There is a picture of Anne Hathaway's cottage in the porch and English fox-hunting scenes in the sitting room.

As it turns out, his wife is a direct descendant of Baba Fareed, a much-venerated Sufi who lived near Lahore; and he himself reveres a Sufi from Lucknow who used to visit his great-grandfather in the 1860s and 1870s.

There was, he said, a trend in modern Islam which claimed that the Sufi tradition was nothing more than reactionary humbug, and heretical to boot, and that Muslims should go back to a more genuine Islam, but that did not sway him in the least. One of his associates, Nizam Khan, who was with us and had perhaps been invited because he has excellent connections in the Sufi world, made it clear that he entirely shared Wajahat's view.

Habibullah is, in fact, the president of the trust which bears his Sufi's name; and, just to illustrate how far Indians are left to make up their own minds about things, he added that he did not even have the authority to invite me to visit the Sufi's shrine. I had, as he put it, to 'get the call' myself.

Millions of Indians still visited Sufi shrines every year, he said. The most popular housed the hair of the Prophet. The tradition was very much alive in India, though not in Pakistan, where Sufi ideas were regarded as so much mumbo-jumbo.

The Sufi tradition, Habibullah went on, had begun in the seventh and eighth centuries, at a time when great Muslim empires – the Umayyad and Abbasid dynasties – controlled large parts of the Middle East and, later, southern Europe.

Muslims of a more spiritual disposition, however, then decided that they wanted nothing to do with courts and caliphs. If they went to courts, they would have to make obeisance to the ruler, when they felt that they should make obeisance only to God. So they shunned worldly life and embraced a philosophy focused on serving the people, because they felt that that is what they had been directed to do by God Himself.

They were ascetics, they always lived in poverty – *suf* is a coarse woollen cloth which Sufis wore to show that they were not interested in the refined things of this world – and they tended to be men of very few words.

Mr Khan, Habibullah went on, had very often taken him to see a Sufi – Baba Gurib Shah Sabir Shishti Rahmatulla, which means the Blessed One – who lived about 100 miles from Delhi, and 'when we were with him, he hardly spoke to me. There were no words, we spoke to each other without talking. He used to be seated on a cushion and he'd motion me to sit next to him. By doing that, he was speaking.' It was, in fact, a sign of particular favour.

The Sufis, said Habibullah, simply kept silence. No one could talk with them, but, although they did not proselytise with words, many of the people who met them became Muslims. They had the quality of sainthood. Khan was clearly just as fervent a believer. The way a Sufi spoke to his followers, he said, was through the eyes and the heart, not by words.

When you came before a living Sufi, you did not look him in the face, his followers only looked at his feet. They could *feel* what he had to say. How many such Sufis were there now in India, I asked? Perhaps 20 or 25, he replied. Thinking of the Delhi area, there was one in Nizamuddin, another in the suburb of Mehrauli and a third near the Ashok Hotel.

As he spoke, it crossed my mind that it might even be possible to see one of these men, if not talk with them. How long would it take to arrange such a meeting, I asked? 'About three days', he replied. Well, I said, that was no good because I was leaving Delhi on the afternoon of the following day.

Mr Khan pursed his lips. Perhaps Kale Baba – which means Black Saint – *might* agree to see me, even at such short notice, if only because Wajahat had once given some pigeons for the shrine where he lived.

Fortunately, he did, and so, next morning, I found myself on the way to Mehrauli in Mr Khan's little car. About 150 yards from the entrance to the shrine, we had to take off our shoes. Given that it was bitingly cold, I was delighted to be able to retain my socks. Mr Khan, however, went in bare feet.

It was clearly a slum area, and poor supplicants sat huddled against the walls of the paved approach road. Dark eyes peered out at us from under their headscarves.

As we got closer to the entrance, there was much bowing and kissing of the ground from Mr Khan. We were met by a man who eventually turned out to be a collector of donations. He told me that Sufis were men to whom God spoke in silence.

A guardian of the shrine indicated that I could not approach the tombs of the 18 Sufis buried there with a bare head. He offered me a white cap in the style of a bus-boy at a fast-food outlet.

Mr Khan indicated that we should pay homage at the tombs before we saw Kale Baba. The first and largest of them, which contains the remains of the greatest of the 18 Sufis, Syed Qutabuddin Bakhtiar Kaki, is a truly magnificent affair. It is fully five metres square under a high, silvery glass dome, and is covered with a green cloth shroud liberally strewn with red and white flowers.

Mr Khan gave me a bunch of flowers so that I might add to their number. He also offered me a rose petal to eat. Meanwhile, he was walking slowly round the tomb, kissing the golden pillars that hold up the dome. Other men were kneeling and praying fervently to receive the blessings of the dead Sufi. Hundreds of pigeons flew restlessly around the courtyard.

Mr Khan then showed me a marble plaque set into the wall and, beside it, a locked, green-painted wooden door. That, he said, was where Baba Fareed used to pray, and this – pointing to the door – was the entrance to his tiny cell. As we left the tombs, he indicated that I should walk backwards, as one might do after an audience of the Queen. No Christian tombs could evoke greater reverence or devotion.

Then it was time to wait upon Kale Baba who fortunately, as it turned out, was willing to speak with other people, even strangers. We climbed marble steps into a small courtyard and there was the Sufi sitting cross-legged on a cushion with a one-bar electric fire against the freezing cold. He had a straggly beard, and was dressed in a grey cloak with a yellow scarf around his head. His eyes were black, fierce and penetrating. I could well understand why Mr Khan had said earlier that he had a reputation for bursts of anger.

When I failed to squat with my feet neatly tucked beneath me, and instead stuck my legs out towards him, Kale Baba looked thoroughly displeased and shooed my feet away. He then relented sufficiently to offer me a cup of tea.

There were two disciples with him, one of whom, as it turned out, was a doctor who spoke some English. Kale Baba is 85 and, as he soon made plain, is thoroughly pleased with his own health and vigour. Rather to my surprise, he pinched the skin on the back of one of my hands, painfully, looked scornfully at the result and then did the same with his own, indicating – via the interpreter – that I was plainly ageing faster than he was. Was he, I wondered, indicating that this evident disparity had spiritual causes?

Anyway, he did the same thing twice to make sure I had got the point. He then said that, when he was 22, he had done the entire *haj*, from Mehrauli to Mecca, on foot, which had taken him six years in all. His real name, the doctor explained, was Mohammed Sharif Shishti. Kale Baba was only his nickname.

The Sufi had never married, the doctor went on, and 'he is not allowing any lady to come into this area. Of course, he prays for ladies, but he is not allowing them to come nearby.' He then proceeded to list the Sufi's virtues. 'He treats everyone the same, be they king or beggar. To him, all people are equal. He does not go to other people's houses even if they invite him.' He himself had been coming to see Kale Baba for 18 years, but the Sufi had never been to his home.

His whole life was dedicated to God. 'When he first came to this place, it was completely broken down, but now he has provided a new mosque which he has painted himself. He will pray for you also.'

What, I asked the Sufi, was the value of silence? 'Only when people are not thinking of material things will peace come to them', he replied, 'I have left the world but not humanity and I can guide people to peace. Love', he added, 'is a kind of peace.'

Did God speak to him, though? 'Of course,' he replied. 'When I pray, I forget myself entirely and feel that God is right there in front of me. No, I have never heard a voice, but thoughts can be God also, and they come to me in silence. When God is happy, what a Sufi says with his tongue are the words of God.'

The audience was now at an end. Again, Kale Baba seemed delighted when he saw that I had difficulty in getting up from my unaccustomed squatting position, and demonstrated that he had no such difficulty.

'You are very lucky to have seen Kale Baba', Mr Khan reassured me. 'God has opened the way for you.' The Sufi shook my hand. He had a vice-like grip. Again, Mr Khan indicated that I should walk backwards as we left. It had been a somewhat bracing encounter.

Absolutely on cue, the collector of donations appeared, and invited us to what might be described as tea with intent. He soon produced a book in which the donations of previous visitors were meticulously recorded.

When I offered him 100 rupees, he indicated displeasure. Most, he pointed out, had given 200 or 500. Shamefaced, I offered 500, still little enough when I thought of the poor waiting at the shrine's gates. 'May God accept your gift', he said piously. As soon as we had left, Mr Khan murmured that the collector was not a full baba, at most only a half-baba. The Sufis, on the other hand, were among the world's super-powers.

I went away reflecting that Kale Baba is certainly no man-pleaser and that saints can come in many guises.

3

Holy men – and women

Very few countries can boast of holy men who attract crowds as large, if not larger, than any rock star. India is one of those few. The wonder is all the greater in that Indians will come, on a regular basis and in huge numbers, not to hear exhilarating music or a hellfire preacher, but a story – and a story with a moral, spiritual or social message at that.

It can be a story woven around the life of the God Krishna or the life of Mahatma Gandhi; but one of the most popular and trusted of India's story-telling holy men, Morari Bapu (bapu simply means spiritual father) takes as his text a version of the Ramayana, an ancient epic poem which is probably the favourite book of most Hindus.

The version which he uses is the work of the great seventeenth-century Indian poet, Tulsi Das and recounts the adventures of both Ram, a prince who is an incarnation of the God Vishnu, and Ram's wife Sita. Its tales have such a hold over the Hindu imagination that, hearing them retold at a *katha*, or story-telling, is in many ways a sort of religious event.

Morari Bapu's *kathas* last for no less than nine days and can attract hundreds of thousands of people. Vast canvas pavilions are set up on an often barren piece of open ground – in summer they are fitted with fans – and, for three or four hours each morning, he takes a small section of the epic and reflects on it in such a way that many of his audience are drawn back again. Over the course of the nine days, he covers the whole story.

At the end of each session, the vast throng are all fed with simple Indian food – rice, dal and vegetable curry. No collections are taken. The people who have asked him to hold the *katha* pay the expenses.

Shortly after lunch, the crowds disperse, often to return the next day. A cynic might say that they have only turned up for a free meal. If so, listening to a discourse of that length while squatting on a carpet or a sheet on the ground is a high price to pay. There really is no such thing as a free lunch.

For one apparently as eloquent as Morari Bapu, the ironic thing, as I discovered when I tracked him down in one of the farther-flung suburbs of Mumbai, is that he has always put an extraordinary value on silence.

I arrived at the block of flats where I had been told he was staying, and found half-a-dozen men putting up a small and colourful pavilion in the back garden for an event later in the day. One of them told me that there were more than half a million people at their last *katha* in Gujerat but, since these were all paid-up devotees, I took the figure with a sizeable pinch of salt.

They all, however, exuded an attractive mixture of reverence and cheerful good humour quite unlike the rather synthetic bonhomie I have encountered at some evangelical Christian gatherings.

With so many people there already, and others arriving all the time, I started to wonder, as I waited, whether the meeting with Bapu was going to be something of a crowd event and not the one-to-one conversation I had been hoping for.

I need not have worried. I was taken up onto the roof of the building and found that he was already waiting on a two-seater garden lounger with a canopy to shield him from the sun. He was dressed entirely in white, with short grey hair and a well-trimmed iron-grey beard and, at 65, looked a picture of glowing good health.

He conveyed no great sense of loftiness, had the most open of faces and, as we talked, gave me the impression of a thoughtful, modest man with no overlay of the sanctimoniousness that is all too common among Indian gurus.

He has been telling his version of the Ramayana ever since he was a teenager, and now holds *kathas* in the United States and Australia (with much smaller numbers) as well as all over India. His charisma and his obvious skill as a storyteller still bring in the crowds in large numbers. Why they all come is a mystery to me. Indians may enjoy a story, particularly a familiar and much-loved one – but for nine days?

Has it something to do with the fact that, according to those who have been to his *kathas*, Morari Bapu does not demand anything from his audience? He does not tell them that they should live in a certain way, go daily to the temple, give money to charity (or himself). In other words, he has no desire to make converts.

What he does do, in his commentary on the story of the Ramayana, is give examples of the best way to live, how to be a good human being. 'He's showing them how to lead the good life,' his daughter

Radhika had told me, 'but in the Indian style, not "you have to do this or that." '

'He also', she went on, 'tells the people who come that they don't have to turn up every day and that, if they fall asleep while he's talking, it doesn't matter at all.' So come they do, to sit at his feet and gather the supposed blessings of being close to a holy man who conveys a sense of peace.

In many ways, the conversation which followed was as mysterious as the idea of half a million people showing up to listen to a story and a holy man's reflections on it. Morari Bapu gave me the impression that, much as he reveres silence, it is still a great mystery to him, a mystery which he is still exploring and to which he does not have all the answers.

Saturday, he said, was always a silent day for him. He also kept silence for a long time in the early morning on the days when he was giving a *katha* and again afterwards. Then, once a year, he took a particular month, often August, and remained silent throughout it.

'I often see people during that time', he said, 'but, when they come, I don't speak at all.' Did they not find that rather embarrassing, I asked? 'On the contrary,' he replied, 'when I am silent, they too become silent. It's a healthy infection!'

When you kept silent for a long time, whatever had been on your mind had a chance to settle down and the dirt was washed away. But, he added, you should never *try* to make that happen. Silence meant no effort. 'If I make an effort,' he said, 'that is interference with the silence.' He quoted a poem by Tulsi Das which said that, in a narrow lane, there was no room for anything else. So it should be with silence.

By this time, 20 or 30 of his followers had arrived on the rooftop and, as the conversation went on, several of them piped up with alternative translations of his answers. They may have been in the presence of their guru, but they were not inhibited in any way.

When he had first started to practise silence 30 years ago, said Bapu, outside noises had disturbed him. The first milestone was when they ceased to trouble him. But the noises, the voices *inside*, still troubled him. Then they too ceased to do so. Finally there was a third milestone when he began to experience complete quietness, inside and out.

But he did not want to make the process sound bland or effortless. There were pitfalls and risks in giving yourself to silence in the way that he had done. 'There is', he said, 'a grave danger that, when you get to that stage, a person – even if he happens to be a saint – can become crazy.'

How, I asked, had he himself coped with that danger? 'At such moments', he replied, 'I need grace from the Lord or, as I would say, The Existence. That is badly needed to keep you in balance. It is grace which adjusts the balance.' Hermit monks might say much the same thing.

These were clearly not glib answers that Bapu had rehearsed a dozen times already. He was sharing the darker side of his own experience.

With these caveats, though, did he feel that God, or The Existence, had communicated with him in the silence? 'Silence', he replied, 'is the door through which God can enter. If you are always talking, talking, you close that door, even though He loves to come. But, in my view, silence is silence, it should be pure and uninterrupted, and

I have so much respect for its power that, if He comes into it, I feel disturbed.'

The notion of God as a kind of unwelcome intruder sounded strange to me. Why on earth, I asked, should he feel disturbed? The reply was blunt and uncompromising. 'I have so much respect for silence that, when I absorb myself into it, I do not need anything more.'

What about Gandhiji, though, and the way he had spoken of being inspired by an inner voice, a voice which gave him the idea of the Salt March and, on one notable occasion, had told him quite clearly that he must fast. When he asked for how long he should fast, the answer had come back equally clearly: '21 days.'

Morari Bapu shook his head. He had never, he said, had that sort of experience. Those who had to lead a nation needed that kind of inspiration in order to help others. He was not, he implied, in the same league as Gandhi. But his own silence was not a stony affair, it flowed, and in it, he believed, other people could feel his joy and the love and warmth which he felt for them.

How, though, did he manage to remain humble when hundreds of thousands came to listen to him? He smiled. 'They come', he said, 'because I am simple and normal, but I just don't know how I remain humble.' He was constantly trying to make it clear to people that he did not want to convert anyone to his way of thinking.

I said I was impressed that he had said he did not know how he remained humble. It was much the same answer the Dalai Lama had given when someone asked him which was the best religion. He too had replied that he did not know. (I wondered when I heard that remark how the Pope or the Archbishop of Canterbury would respond to the same question.)

'We have sacred books,' said Bapu, 'and in one of the Upanishads it says that those who claim to know, know nothing, but those who say they don't know, know everything.'

When he was speaking in a *katha*, he added, remarkable things often happened which he did not claim to understand. 'I'm not 100 per cent sure but, when I talk continuously for three or four hours, I often feel as if I'm in a state of silence.' How on earth did he explain that?

Sufi mystics, he replied, experienced the same thing. They would be speaking to their disciples but have the feeling that someone else was speaking through them. He had felt the same. It was as much a mystery to him as it would be to me. Silence might seem like nothingness, yet it was the most important thing in the world.

So here was a holy man with no pretence or guile, who made no fanciful claims for himself and did not profess to know all the answers. He was very far from the self-promoting super-guru I had been expecting. An honest Indian, or so it seemed to me.

There are other honest Indians who would not dream of calling themselves holy men but who practise silence in a rather less intensive way. Rajmohan Gandhi, who currently teaches in a mid-western American university and is the author of an outstanding biography of his grandfather the Mahatma, is one of them.

'When I enter a period of silence, which is not all that often or for very long, perhaps five, ten, twenty minutes,' he said, 'in the first few moments I am aware of burdens and anxieties, so those opening moments are often troubling ones. Almost always, however, those feelings subside and something very different takes over – a sense of peace, calm and often assurance.'

'Often, too, a sense of compassion comes, and I start thinking of others in a good way, not as if they were a burden to me. People you would like good things to happen to, you think what you could do for them. So the silence then becomes peace-giving, hope-giving, strength-giving.'

'There are moments when I feel silence is a better communicator than the spoken or written word. I don't know but, in it, I feel a nearness to people, a oneness with them, a sensitivity to them. I'm still trying to figure it out but I guess it is because, in a way, it's a three-way affair – God and other people and me. Perhaps, with an openness to God, the connection with others becomes stronger. I have a keener insight into them than if we were talking.'

'In that silence, so many of my prejudices and preconceptions fade away. I seem to see other people more clearly and respectfully and I become more conscious of their virtues and strengths, which I had previously been confused about.'

'I have ceased to ask myself whether any of my thoughts come from God. My search is as to whether my thoughts seem good, right and helpful rather than whether they are from Him. If you press me, I imagine that they are sometimes from God, but it's not a claim I'd wish to make.'

'Actually, I tend to get my most inspired thoughts when I'm walking and reflecting, which is surprising because, while walking, I also have to concentrate both to make sure I'm going in the right direction and to avoid the ice in case I fall and break a hip. The number of times that the resolution of some historical or academic or practical question has come to me with amazing clarity while I'm walking is quite astonishing. It happens again and again.'

'Occasionally, during times of silence, I've thought I heard a voice and I have perhaps felt a tap on the wrist two or three times. What sort of person would I be without my times of silence? Far more confused, far more dissatisfied, far pricklier. My gosh, yes, silence is a boon! It's underrated and unacknowledged and yet it is still there, humble and waiting to serve.'

Indian holy men have had a very extensive press, for good and ill. Their female counterparts have made fewer waves. Were they, I wondered, any less convinced about the value of silence? Who better to ask than the 30 Hindu nuns at the Paunar ashram which Gandhi's greatest disciple, Vinoba Bhave, founded near Wardha in the middle of India?

I did not expect them to be any less enthusiastic than the men I had talked to, but I was quite unprepared for the torrent of exuberance that greeted me there.

Arriving by taxi from Nagpur, I found a cluster of low buildings around a large and rather overgrown vegetable patch. The welcome, from the male administrator, Gautam Bajaj, was warm, but I got quite a shock when I was taken to my guest room.

There was no towel (only on request), no hot water, no mirror, no toilet paper, only a bare bulb for light, and a stern, unyielding palliasse for a bed. Even the soap was of the home-made variety – the bought version, Bajaj explained, often contained beef tallow.

There was no pampering in the dining room either. Breakfast the next morning consisted of a cold, semolina-like substance, the previous day's broken-up chapattis and a small bowl of hot milk.

'What bizarre food!', I observed to the nun beside me. She smiled. 'It is to help our spiritual practise', she replied. 'Holy food!', snapped a second nun. I did not, somehow, find that entirely convincing.

'I know what you are missing', said a third lady brightly. 'You need a cup of tea', and promptly made me one. Most of the nuns eat their food squatting on the floor, and everyone, guests included, washes up their own dishes, using – believe it or not – wood ash. You live and learn.

It is not only hard going for the guests. The nuns do not spare themselves either. They rise at 4 a.m. and lights out is at 8.30 every evening. They make and wash their own clothes, do their own house cleaning and grow their own vegetables. They seldom go to the local market except for basic items such as salt.

Each of the nuns takes all the 11 vows prescribed by Mahatma Gandhi – celibacy, voluntary poverty, non-violence and so on – but they do not include a vow of obedience to some higher earthly authority. 'Nowhere in India', said one nun, 'is there a vow of obedience. Our concept of religion is that a person should be totally independent. Religion should make you free in every sense of the word.'

Later, an elderly nun took me aside. 'You should know', she said, 'that everyone is independent here. There is no one in charge, no abbot, no director. We eat where we wish and go to the times of prayer or not, as we choose. We have complete freedom.'

It is quite unlike any monastic rule I have ever come across, but it seems to work. I have never come across a livelier or more contented group of women. Their chanting in the darkness before dawn is still ringing in my ears.

I call on a spectacularly ebullient nun, Pravina Desai, and we talk sitting in her little garden. She is the daughter of a High Court barrister and has been at Paunar for 47 years. Ever since she was five years old, she said, she had been longing for a real relationship with God, and could not wait to become a nun.

The rishis, she said, had stipulated two ideal times for silent meditation. The first began at 4 in the morning, about an hour and a half before the sunrise. At that point, the whole ozonosphere – the layer of atmosphere where ozone is formed – came down closer to us, and the effect was very invigorating and refreshing. The second time the rishis had recommended was from 6 to 7.30 in the evening, and then you could watch the sun setting.

'What comes in those times', said Pravina, 'depends on your faith. If we have faith in ourselves, that faith and confidence increases tremendously as you meditate. If you have faith in the universe, you are given the courage to stand against anything which is not proper and truthful.

'What comes is soul-power and you realise that which is God in your body, soul and intellect. Something sparkles, something which is not earthly at all. It is not a sensual, mental or emotional experience and it has nothing to do with modern life. It is a step into another world.'

But wasn't it boring just sitting there? 'Boring!', Pravina exploded, 'my goodness, you could spend the whole day in that way, it is charming, enchanting, delightful, blissful. Silence is always happier than speech. I just love to sit. I am waiting for those hours to come. When you meditate in the right way, silence always communicates and it is always graceful.'

Nor was it a selfish pastime. She wanted, she said, to meditate in such a way that non-violence came to have a greater power in the world than those who could push the nuclear button. That was always her prayer.

As for whether God spoke to her, she always had to think carefully about what He did in her thought system. It was quite rare for her to get intuitions but, when she did, she followed them blindly. It was apt to happen at the beginning of some big project. It was just different from ordinary thought, it didn't belong to this world, it had a supernatural quality.

'We in India', she went on, 'believe that there is a noosphere (often defined as the sphere of human thought) and that in it is preserved the practical and spiritual wisdom of humanity, the lessons which our forefathers – among them the great men and women of the world – have learnt. When you meditate in silence, the fruits of that wisdom can convey themselves to you.'

In other words, Pravina was claiming that she – and, indeed, anyone who meditated in the right spirit – could tap into the inherited wisdom of the human race. It is, to put it mildly, an extraordinary idea, but then she has a poetic concept of silence and poets are allowed apparently extravagant notions that may hold within them a kernel of truth.

In the Indian scriptures, she said, silence was not something that had to do with speech, it was a quality of the mind. She might speak, but, inside, she should be 'like ice, cool, sweet and balanced'. Balance was not possible without silence.

'What we see and feel with our senses is totally ephemeral, in continuous flux. Truth, on the other hand, is permanent, and that is what we have to seek. If we are to do that, silence and balance are crucial – and, for me, silence is the most valuable thing in the world.'

Still trying to ponder the meaning of what Pravina had said to me, I encountered another remarkable nun called Usha, which means dawn. She is 80 years old, and has a calmness and grace which it is impossible to miss. Like Pravina, she has poetry in her spirit.

'Silence', she began, 'means entering the great cave of the heart. In silence, I find glimpses of God, but words are too feeble to express it. Vinoba, you know, practised silent prayer when 100,000 people were present. He did it for years. In that common silence there was no problem of religion, caste or language. His formula was M2A – two parts meditation, one part action.'

She had been thinking about the book I was writing, and had had the thought that speech which came out of silent meditation had a quality of eternity about it. Not speaking conquered the senses, not thinking conquered the mind, and, when the mind was empty, something sprang up and floated in the air. When we had no desires, we merged with God.

Usha then introduced me to a third nun who had recently been silent for a whole year, and had communicated with other people only in writing.

She was a quiet, rather shy lady, and I asked her the obvious question: why had she decided to keep silent for so long? 'It was not my decision', she replied. 'I felt this voice which came from inside telling me clearly that I should observe total silence for a year, I don't know why, perhaps it had something to do with my inner development, but I accepted because I felt it was coming from Him.'

'For that reason, I didn't find any difficulty in doing it. If, on the other hand, I had decided for myself to do it, I would have found it hard. Sometimes, I hear that inner voice telling me something I don't really welcome, but I always obey. It is not like a sound, it is hard to describe but it has a different quality about it.'

'One day, 25 years ago, I woke up one morning and felt that same presence. It bowed to me and told me that, from that moment, I must never touch money again. I accepted, although I have no natural instinct in that direction. Again, it was the inner voice and I found it easy to accept for that reason.'

'I have found that there are intuitions and then there is a voice. Intuitions come more often, though they are not a daily experience for me, the voice only at very special moments. It must, I feel, be obeyed. If I decided not to take salt in my food,' she explained, 'it would not long sustain me.' The inner voice is her salt.

Before she left me, the nun asked me not to mention her name. What she had shared with me, she explained, was not a secret but it was sacred.

As I left Paunar, I had to admit that attractive food might not be quite as important as I had imagined.

4

Playing with silence

How on earth do you begin to talk about silence to people whose whole lives seem to be about making a noise? It was surely, I thought, the last thing that musicians and teachers of music would want to waste their time on. Yet, as it turned out, it was something they could not wait to talk about – and not merely as some minor, peripheral topic but as a mysterious, almost magical element on which the entire practise of their art depends.

When I called the Royal College of Music in London to ask if anyone, anyone at all, would be interested to speak about the place of silence in music, I expected a tepid response, if any. I could not have been more wrong. Within hours, 15 professors, teachers and performers had responded. They positively tumbled over themselves to express their eagerness to talk about the importance of silence.

'Silence', said Stephen Varcoe, a baritone who teaches singing at the College, 'is extremely important in music. It is not only a lack of sound. It is the canvas on which the whole thing is painted.'

'The silences within music', said Roger Vignoles, an accompanist who has toured with Kiri te Kanawa, 'are incredibly important.

Silence properly felt and understood by a performer takes an audience deeper into the meaning of a work than the notes do.'

'In music,' said Julian Jacobson, a professor of piano and chamber music, 'silence is absolutely vital. It is not anti-music, it is an essential part of the musical discourse. If there were no reverence for silence, the music would be dead, it would just be continuous noise.'

This torrent of conviction left no room for doubt that silence is crucially important, in classical music at least. Everyone I spoke to at the Royal College regarded it as much, much more than a mere absence of sound.

Without exception, they spoke almost reverently of an element which, to them, is as potent as the notes themselves, an element which has to be performed just as sensitively and delicately, or else the music loses its soul. At times, as they spoke, it sounded as if silence had a life of is own, as if it were a presence and not simply an absence.

'I always think of silence as a flower bed, an environment out of which beautiful things can grow', said Mark Messenger, the head of strings at the College. 'The flower bed in our age is full of weeds because of the chatter that goes on all the time but, in a concert hall, the weeds are not there, it's one of the very few places in the West where you can experience profound silence. There, you have a chance to realise the importance of the silence from which a piece of music comes and into which it goes.

'The silence before and after a performance is an integral part of any piece of music. The piece starts before the first note is played. There is a preparation, an anticipation, a kind of receptiveness that something amazing is about to happen – and a great performer will know instinctively the exact moment at which the music is meant to start.'

In his experience, said Julian Jacobson, young performers often started to play too soon. He remembered going to a concert at the Festival Hall in the 1960s where Sviatislav Richter was to play the Liszt B Flat piano sonata. It was the first time Richter had been allowed to come to the West, and the concert was a sell-out.

'Richter came into the hall', recalled Jacobson, 'and he sat at the keyboard for at least three minutes before he began. In a way, it was terrifying. He wasn't going to start until he was totally prepared and the audience was totally ready. It was a real relief when he started to play. There is only one moment when it is right to begin.'

Nor is it simply a matter of knowing when to break the silence, because that silence is also a crucial element in the music itself. 'Some of the greatest pieces', said Roger Vignoles, 'are actually depictions of silence. Take, for example, one of Schubert's songs, "Der Doppelgänger" [The Double] which starts with long, slow chords in the piano part.'

'Then the singer comes in 'Still ist die Nacht, Ruhend die Gasse' [Still is the night, quiet the streets] and, whenever I play that, I'm deeply conscious that I'm playing an incredibly palpable silence. The musical pulse is like a heartbeat and, when that heartbeat is suspended, it gives the music the quality of profound silence.'

'In playing that song, the silence surrounding the music is vital. If someone knocked over a music stand at that point, the whole meaning of the piece would be shattered. When I'm playing the introduction to the song, I am of course listening to the sound I'm creating, but I'm also listening equally intently to the silence which precedes it, and to the silence created by the audience which envelopes the whole occasion.'

'If I'm rehearsing the song at home with a singer, we are both exploring and feeling the silence around the piece, but that silence is as nothing compared with the intensity of the surrounding silence when there are 500 people waiting with bated breath to listen to it.'

'In that sense, the music is incredibly intensified by the number of people listening to it, and the silence they themselves create. In that silence, complex and profound pieces of communication are going on all the time between the performers and the audience.'

'Performers are acutely aware of their audience – they're aware of them because of the *quality* of the silence while they're playing. Many years ago, I remember doing a morning concert at the Bath Festival, and the singer and I both found it hard work, because we sensed that we'd never got full attention. All we knew was that we both felt that the audience was not really with us.'

'After the concert had finished, we walked back through the room where we'd been performing. People said how fantastic and wonderful it had been, and they obviously meant it. Then we discovered that the building we were playing in had a wooden frame, it was a very windy day and it was creaking continuously. We realised that it was the tiny creaks we had both registered sub-consciously as restlessness on the part of the audience.'

You could not overstate the importance of the silences within music, he went on. That was not just in what was called a 'general pause', when everyone was waiting for something to happen, but even in the articulation of the music.

'Let's take, for example, the passage in Mozart's *Così fan Tutte* where the two young men, Ferrando and Guglielmo, come in to tell the two girls, Dorabella and Fiordiligi, that they have to go away to war. It isn't true, of course, it's just part of an elaborate plot to test the girls' fidelity.'

'They come in to this hesitant music punctuated by orchestral chords played staccato and it's the gaps, the hesitations, the silences between the chords which are most expressive of the emotions that are there – the mock-sadness and mock-hesitancy.'

'They are the most incredibly poignant kind of silences. If you don't take care of the silences between the chords, the result is flat and meaningless. The silences are actually more meaningful than either the words or the notes.'

It is exactly the same in popular music. Tom Wakeley, a vocal coach at the Royal Academy of Dramatic Art for more than 20 years, illustrated the point at the piano. He sang the opening line of the tune which made Judy Garland's name, 'Somewhere over the Rainbow'. 'Now,' he said, 'if you don't have a pause after that before you sing "way up high", it just doesn't have the same effect.'

'Then take a song from the musical *The Life* with music by Cy Coleman. It begins "He's no good but I'm" and then you *must* have a pause before "no good without him." In that moment of silence, the singer's thought process is relayed to an audience. Something magical happens in that moment of communication.'

It is in such silences that an audience is drawn more deeply into the music. 'Their rapport with a piece', said Professor David Ward, who has taught piano at the Royal College for 40 years, 'flowers and flourishes in the silences. By its very nature, silence calls forth reflection. That's one reason why it is so potent. Music is not all about sound.'

Silence within music, in other words, is a sort of second language, no less potent than the language of sound, and understood just as clearly as the first language by an audience. If that second language is not articulated as well as the first, then a performance is going to be either second-rate or a thoroughgoing flop. In other words, a good performer needs to be musically bilingual.

'When we converse,' said Mark Messenger, 'there is a natural speech pattern, hesitancy mixed with a fluency which underpins the meaning of what we have to say. In the same way, a great composer uses silence as part of the musical narrative. The problem comes when a work is played by people who are not great performers. Then the silences can so easily become an empty space rather than part of the narrative.'

'One of the reasons for that is the compulsion of mediocre musicians to count the length of a silence rather than feeling it. I just wish musicians would take more notice of the way great actors use silence. They don't *count* their way through Shakespeare!'

'Take the last movement of the Mozart E Flat Major string quartet. The opening figure of the last movement has two quavers with a crochet rest, and that is then repeated. So often you hear it played metrically, and then the rests are merely a blank space in the music. That way the silence means nothing. Silence must not be just a dutiful rendering of the score, it must be a full part of the *spirit* of the music.'

It also had to be handled flexibly, or your silent companions in this musical conversation – the audience – were going to be less than delighted. 'As soon as you start to count,' Messenger went on, 'the silence becomes an absolute metric gap. With a composer who uses it really well, like Mozart, it is such an integral part of his music that the length of the silence can only be determined in the moment of performance, in the context of what has happened before or what's about to happen. Again, you've got to *feel* it.'

'Silence is a critically important constituent of any piece of music, and the penalty of not handling it well is the same as not being creative in the way you play the notes – the audience will be neither convinced nor engaged. You have to *relish* the silence as much as the sounds.'

Nor is that second language something that can be learned by rote or diligent application. It is a language that cannot, in the last resort, be taught. It is a language of the heart, which comes to a musician only through artistic instinct – and the young do not always find it easy to come by.

'One of the things young musicians find hardest', said Roger Vignoles, 'is to give time for silence in the music. They always tend to rush, they seem to feel uncomfortable with the silence and, as a result, don't let the music breathe. It's partly nervousness and partly the spirit of the age.'

'The young do tend to see music just in terms of notes', agreed Julian Jacobson. 'They need to be bullied into understanding the tensions and the releases in the music, to make a proper use of silence. The have to be guided into not making it just a mechanical performance of notes.'

They often needed to be reminded of the *bon mot* of the great pianist Artur Schnabel: 'The notes I handle no better than many pianists, but the pauses between the notes ... ah, that is where the art resides!'

'I encourage students to listen to the *silence* when they are playing', said David Ward. 'I ask them what they do during the rests and they usually reply "count." So I say "but if you don't listen to it, a silent bar or moment doesn't have any meaning."'

'They have a fear of the silent moments in the music. Often, students just want to fill it up. What worries them is that they've got nothing to do. They get embarrassed or anxious and they say "what do I do now?"!' All of which does sound a little severe on the poor learners, but the College is expected to produce exceptional musicians.

If the silent conversation between performers and audience has been a fruitful one, the reward often comes either in terms of silence or the absence of it. 'The other evening', said Mark Messenger, 'I was conducting Shostakovich's Choral Symphony, which is a trans-position of his Eighth string quartet – and listening to it, you are taken through an amazing emotional journey, ending with resig-nation and hopelessness.

'When we'd finished, the audience did not want to clap and it was at least half a minute before anyone did so. So much was said in that silence. The audience had been taken out of their comfort zones, out of the emotional atmosphere of their twenty-first-century lives. The silence made them realise that they hadn't just been listening to a piece of music, they had shared in some measure the emotions Shostakovich felt in his time, and that silence became part of their experience of that emotional journey.

'On the other hand, if you take an exciting piece, like Beethoven's

Seventh for example, the excitement is such, especially in the last movement, that you can't help being roused to an immediate response. In that case, silence at the end would be a painful thing for the performers.'

The place of silence in music over the centuries has a curious trajectory. In the religious music of the Middle Ages, and Gregorian chant in particular, there were silences whose purpose was to add resonance to the words.

'After each phrase', said Jean-Philippe Calvin, professor of academic studies at the Royal College, 'there was a very deliberate pause, so that the text could be reflected on, so that the memory of it could seep into the soul.'

In the Chinese and Japanese music of the same period, somewhat influenced by the philosophy of Zen, there were even longer and more meaningful silences. In Noh theatre, which developed in the fifteenth century or possibly even earlier and which used themes from religious stories and myths, there was the same idea of observing silence so that the story's spiritual meaning could sink in. 'With its musical accompaniment', said Calvin, 'Noh drama is almost a religious event like a Mass.'

Then, in the West at least, he went on, we had totally lost the notion of reflective silence in music. With Bach, the idea was that music should be continuous. Although Bach himself was deeply religious, he made silence less important, as it remained in many ways for several centuries.

It was not that silence disappeared from music, merely that the notion of its spiritual value was lost. The great composers of the next centuries saw it as more of a dramatic device. Haydn was a master at checking the momentum of a piece with a pause which made you wonder what was coming next. Mozart used silence brilliantly to heighten the drama and create expectations. For Beethoven, it was the perfect way to build and hold tension.

'You also', Calvin went on, 'have to take account of the fact that, in the eighteenth century, people chattered away to each other during concerts. The music was rather in the background, there was no particular respect for silence. That's quite different to how things are now, with audiences listening religiously in total silence.'

In recent years, however, an older tradition had begun to reassert itself. 'After centuries of continuous music', said Calvin, 'we have come back to the notion of silence as something which has spiritual and religious significance.'

There were composers such as the Estonian, Arvo Pärt, a deeply spiritual man who had decided to study mediaeval music. As a result, some of his pieces had the character of silent prayers. Sophia Gubadailina from Kazakhstan and the Georgian Giya Kanchelli had both produced pieces called Night Prayers. And, in England, John Tavener – one of whose pieces is called Towards Silence – clearly had a conviction of its spiritual value. All his pieces had periods of literal silence, when the music stops, and he usually specified for how many seconds the silence should last.

'For all of these composers', said Calvin, 'the meaning of silence is very spiritual, a chance to reflect on the celestial harmony.'

Other modern composers had approached silence from an entirely different point of view. The New York school, and particularly men like Morton Feldman, had rebelled passionately against the tradition of continuous sound and spoke about wanting to 'unglue the music', said Calvin.

John Cage, an American much influenced by Zen, was equally radical. 'In 1950', Calvin went on, 'he went to Harvard and sat in their anechoic (echoless) chamber where there was supposed to be virtually no sound.

'When he came out, he told the engineer that he had, in fact, heard two kinds of sound, one very high-pitched, the other low. The engineer told him that the high-pitched sound was his nervous system at work, the low sound the noise of his blood circulating. At that moment, Cage understood that there was no such thing as absolute silence.'

He then thought of producing an entirely silent piece of 'music'. When the idea first occurred to him, he gave it the working title Silent Prayers. As a younger man, he had intended to study theology and became a minister. Four years later, he came up with a piece simply entitled '4' 33"', whose length was decided by throwing a dice. He intended it as a demonstration of the non-existence of silence, of the permanent presence of all the sounds around us. The first performance took place at Woodstock in New York State in 1952.

It had been a remarkable occasion. 'A very fine pianist, David Tudor, came onto the stage', said Calvin, 'with a stop watch and a score which was blank except for the words "4' 33" *tacet*" [it is silent].' Tudor opened the lid of the piano and did nothing except close it and then reopen it to indicate the length of the movements into which Cage had divided the piece. He was there purely to perform the silence.

'The people in the audience, of course, had come psychologically prepared to hear music, but they heard nothing. After half a minute, they started to murmur, after a minute they were saying to themselves "just what is going on here?" By the third minute they had begun talking to each other and by the fourth some of them were shouting, almost as if they wanted to tar and feather Cage.'

That, so far as Cage was concerned, was living proof that there is no such thing as silence. He had always wanted to include sounds from the environment and, in that, too, he had succeeded triumphantly. He had, for a few brief moments, replaced continuous music with a very different kind of sound, the noise of a puzzled and enraged audience. His Zen master must have been delighted.

5

No words, please

Strange – or perhaps not so strange – that it should take a visit to a place of silence to make me reflect on what we use words for.

I arrived at Gethsemani, the Trappist monastery in Kentucky where the much-celebrated monk Thomas Merton spent so many years, and was greeted by a volley of injunctions to remain silent.

'Silence beyond this point' at the beginning of the path which leads down to the monastery buildings; 'silence in this walkway' at the approach to the abbey church; 'silence is spoken here' in the dining room; 'no talking in this garden' and 'silence please' outside the guest rooms.

So blunt, so peremptory, there were no exclamation marks on the notices, but I felt as if there ought to be. They were like a slap in the face, like being suddenly gagged or muffled, like being stripped of one of one's basic faculties. By their repetition and insistence, they conveyed a sense of oppression, rather than one of freedom, a sense of being bullied, shackled.

I had come, like the people who were already there on retreat, from a world of noise and speech. Speech is how we express our opinions and reactions, the way in which we display so much that we believe is good about us – our sense of humour, our (of course!) shrewd insights, our impressive judgements.

It is the way in which we establish our identity and status with both our competitors and our friends and acquaintances. It is, in other words, the way in which we sell ourselves to people.

Words are our resource and our weapon in the ebb and flow of daily life. They are the stuff of social interchange, of human friendship. They are also a carapace that we construct to defend the (often bogus) picture of ourselves which we present to other people. People such as myself sometimes feel proud of how well we use words – except at those times when we forget what it was that we wanted to say!

Suddenly, for much of the time in this place, I could use them no more. I sat opposite a woman at supper whom I had never seen before, and we had no way of introducing ourselves to each other. The rules were so strict that even eye-contact would have felt like an intrusion. If I had smiled, it would have seemed as if I were propositioning her. It was remarkably uncomfortable and did not make you want to linger over your food.

Curiously, a monk spoke on tape while we ate, clearly intending to fill the void with wholesome thoughts. He waffled a good deal, almost making a case for silence by the way he spoke, but argued that silence can be both worship and an act of penance. That struck a chord because having to remain silent in those early moments in Gethsemani did seem to me rather like a penance.

There is no doubt that silence transforms the nature of human relationships. It leaves us puzzled, at first, as to how we should communicate with each other. It strips us of all the verbiage with which we habitually garland ourselves and leaves us, in a sense, naked.

Thus exposed, we have to relate to other people just as we are. It brings us back, in some measure, to the core of ourselves, to a place where we have to communicate in the second language that is so important to musicians. I think of my friend Catherine, a young married woman, who came away from a retreat during which she had never spoken to any of her group but feeling – she said – far more love for them all than if they had spent the entire week chatting together.

Silence also takes away the power which words have to divide us from our fellow human beings. Speech can so easily become an instrument of separation but, speechless as we were for the moment, I had no idea whether these other people shared my political opinions, my enthusiasms or the vast range of my prejudices – which might, I have to confess, have helped decide whether I liked them or not.

In silence, there are fewer of the prickly hazards that can stop us from forming congenial relationships. In silence, there is more chance that I might feel a basic sympathy towards the others, because their humanity and perhaps mine is plain and unvarnished. As we all know, there is always a simpler, needier self lurking behind the undergrowth of words.

Suddenly, I began to warm to the idea of spending a few days in relative silence. I did not have to put myself about with the usual obligatory chit-chat, words which often mean nothing in particular, and that was a rather relaxing thing in itself. And if there was none of the pleasure that can come from the social intercourse of speech, there were also fewer of the irritations.

We had laid aside the tool with which we normally try to please or impress people and, when we helped or were helped by someone, in the kitchen or dining room, there was something uncluttered about the exchange,

At breakfast and in meals generally, the obligatory silence also took away the importance of who was sitting with whom, since everyone was equally uncommunicative. It abolished any notion of hierarchy and diminished the cloying power of special relationships.

As notices in the elevators pointed out, the silence was intended to be an aid to prayer and reflection, and one hoped that it was. I presume the central point of the exercise was that it left you alone, standing before God, without any distractions, especially of the human kind.

The retreaters were mostly, though not exclusively, of a certain age. Heaven alone knows what predicaments and problems they had brought to Gethsemani – what anxieties, what sadnesses, what family tragedies, what puzzlements. They had come to still the torrent of their emotions, confront any guilt, deepen their spiritual journey and to seek from the silence, the worship and the advice of the monks, solace of some kind.

They had all come hoping that the silence would not only help them to confront the issues they faced but that, from it, a divine voice or nudge or murmur would emerge to lead them forth from their anxieties.

When we met in places where we *were* allowed to speak, it was easy enough to find out why they had come to Gethsemani. This was America, so there was little of the reserve that you might find in Europe and, in any case, the silent zone was limited to the core of the retreat centre. Even there, indeed, there was a dining area where speaking was permitted.

On the little hill above the monastery, looking out across the rolling, wooded meadows of Kentucky, I met a divorced man called Dan, a computer analyst from Indiana. I had already noticed him during one of the services in the abbey church, standing in the stalls with the monks, and had thought it odd that he should be wearing ordinary clothes while they were all in their habits.

It turned out that he was a postulant who was thinking of becoming a monk because he was so distraught about what the cacophony of American life, the lack of any notion of silence, was doing to his four offspring, all of them now in their late teens or twenties.

How such a retreat from the world was supposed to help them was not immediately obvious, but Dan clearly had a sense that, by that dramatic act of surrender, by giving himself to a life of prayer and silence, he might persuade them to rethink their lives. He had already spent some time at another monastery and had come to Gethsemani to have a second 'live-in experience' with a monastic community.

His anxieties about his children poured out of him. They always, he said, had to have some purveyor of noise in their ears, when he met them they did not seem to be present, they had no idea of silence, they were driven by noise and a constant need for distraction. They were being spiritually disabled by over-stimulation.

'You go on a car trip with them and, as soon as we start, they plug their iPods into the stereo system and, with 10,000 songs to choose from, they flip from one to the next even before the last one has finished. When I took a car trip as a kid – and there were eight of us in the family – the radio wasn't on, we'd say a rosary, we'd all be silent and then we'd play games like spotting letters on the stop signs.'

'If you asked my kids what they'd lost, they'd say nothing has been taken away from them, but I'd say they've lost any understanding of who they are. How do you get to know yourself if you don't bother to stop and have thoughts? They know all there is to know about keeping up their physical health, but their spiritual health is something else again. When I think of my children's spiritual demise, I feel guilty.'

'They don't ever stop to be with themselves, it's as if they are afraid of taking time to do that. They have to have noise to protect them from themselves. They're afraid that, if they tried silence, they'd find out things they don't want to hear. They're afraid they'd discover a spiritual dimension to life that they don't want to have to deal with – and they want to keep it at bay.'

Dan's diagnosis of the spiritual state of his offspring is remarkably similar to the prophetic things that the great psychiatrist Carl Jung had to say in a letter of 1957 to a man planning to start a campaign against noise.

People, Jung wrote, became as habituated to noise as they were to over-indulgence in alcohol and, 'just as you pay for this with cirrhosis of the liver, so in the end you pay for nervous stress with a premature depletion of your vital substance.' With children, so much was fed into them from the outside that they no longer thought of something they could do from inside themselves.

He believed, Jung went on, that there was a widespread though not conscious fear which loved noise because it stopped that fear from being heard. 'Noise is welcome because it drowns the inner instinctive warning. Fear seeks noisy company and pandemonium to scare away the demons. Noise, like crowds, gives a feeling of security, therefore people love it ... noise protects us from painful reflection, it scatters our anxious dreams. It assures us that we are all in the same boat.'

'We wouldn't have noise if we didn't secretly want it. ... If there were silence, ... the real fear is what might come up from one's depths – all the things that have been held at bay by noise.

'The more you attack noise,' Jung warned his correspondent, 'the closer you come to the taboo territory of silence, which is most dreaded. There are far more people than one supposes who are not disturbed by noise, for they have nothing in them that could be disturbed. Noise is an integral component of modern "civilisation." It is an evil with deep roots ... it all goes with the spiritual disorientation of our time.'

Twana, a 34-year-old African-American who stages fashion shows in Ashville, North Carolina, lives cheek-by-jowl with that disorientation day in and day out, and had fled to Gethsemani to get away from it. She had endured a 16-hour bus journey to be there for just two days and was revelling in every precious second.

'There are lots of dragons, elves and witches in my world,' she said, 'and I need to protect myself spiritually, to regain the joy I once had. I have to get away, to change my whole venue, to be alone with my Creator.'

'When I'm at home, people come and talk to me all the time, I'm always getting their ego, it's always the same problems, so monotonous it drives you nuts, and it's always about everything that doesn't matter, all the distractions that people get tied up with – so the silence here is wonderful.'

'In the world I'm in I feel I'm losing brain cells. I showcase talent and they're always wanting another show. I wonder what the people who appear in them really want – are they thinking about getting their next big screen TV or what's going on in the core of them?'

'We have a system in this country which is created to strip you of one thing, spirit, so then you become empty shells. The whole thing is based on systematic distraction. We have freedom, but we're still slaves to one thing or another.'

So many of the people I met at Gethsemani gave me a sense that they were living in a world short of oxygen and that they were coming up for air. 'There's far too much talking in college,' said a post-graduate student from the University of Virginia, 'and it's because they're afraid of being with themselves.' What did she think of silence, I asked Carol from Alton, Illinois? 'Liberating', she replied, beaming.

'All the racket out there', said Peake, a former teacher of English, 'is a kind of distraction. If I'm distracted, I don't have to think about anything. But, if you need distraction, just what is it that you're being distracted from?'

All of them had escaped, for a few brief days, from the deluge of noise that engulfs America and much of the developed world. It is a universe where sound, like sex, sells, a world which steers its citizens imperiously, determinedly, towards their external selves and their material needs. To Father Damian, the guestmaster at Gethsemani, it seems as if American TV is '60 per cent selling and not entertainment'.

The truth is that capitalism flourishes best in a society whose members are driven by impulse rather than reflection, in which there is little or no material profit. Wall Street, Walmart and the rest of corporate America naturally have no interest in the inner needs of their clients, except in so far as they affect the sales figures or the God-almighty stock market indices. The American dream, in any case, is far more about accessing riches from without than seeking any riches that may lie within.

So the retreaters come, 160 every month, their numbers increasing all the time because, as the assistant guestmaster, Father Carlos, puts it, 'they can't any longer hear what life is all about, the noise is so great.'

In the economic recession, reservations for their 56 guest rooms had shot up. People said they needed to reassess their lives, to decide what was important and what was not. They came to look at life in a way they had not tried before, to soak themselves in another world and another way.

Most of them, said Carlos, had never tried silence and some did not stay the course. They were supposed to be at Gethsemani from Monday to Friday, but a number left on Tuesday and rang later to say that they just were not ready for so much silence.

What, though, of the 47 monks at Gethsemani, which is the oldest working monastery in the United States, founded as it was in 1848? How had Carlos and his brothers been affected by changing times and the ever-increasing torrent of external noise? Their numbers have gone down – at the peak, there were 270 monks – even though the severities of former days have been substantially eased.

'Silence is pretty much intact and we don't talk in the monastery,' said Father Carlos, 'but if you are assigned a job, you obviously need to be given instructions. We also have talking rooms now, where a monk can spend time in conversation with one of his brothers. Those rooms, of course, are not just for shooting the breeze, there has to be a reason for the meeting which helps both of them.'

Brother Paul has been at Gethsemani long enough to have had Thomas Merton – who died in 1968 – as his novice master. We walked together the half mile or so down stony tracks to the hermitage which the monastery had had built for Merton in 1960.

A maple and a tulip poplar stand guard beside the simple building. There is a giant, rough-hewn Cross and, over to the right, a statue of the Blessed Virgin. I sat on Merton's old seat, which he called his Bench of Dreams, as Paul told me of the changes that had transformed monastic life at Gethsemani.

'There used to be', he said, 'a great culture of silence in the monastery, but today it's hardly mentioned. The newer people who've come don't have the same rigorous practice of silence. In the past, you could follow a conversation between two monks across a room because they talked in sign language – there was even a dictionary of those signs – but things are quite different now.

'We don't get Facebook or Twitter on our systems, our servers cut them out, but I'm on Twitter myself, because I write haikus every day and they're out there.' Different indeed!

Dan, the postulant, who had only been at Gethsemani for a few days but had seen something of life within the monastery, also felt that there had been a considerable relaxation. There was silence in the monastery's halls, he said, but when they all went out together to work on its 2,000-acre estate, the monks laughed and joked together.

That is not the only thing that has changed. 'In the old days', said Father Damian, who arrived at Gethsemani in 1978, 'silence was a mechanical thing, taken for granted, everything was very strict until the Vatican Council in the 1960s.'

'For example, you were supposed to accuse people if you saw something wrong in them, breaking a rule or forgetting to do something. There'd then be what was called a proclamation, the accused had to stand in front of the abbot and he'd usually be given a penance.

'That, of course, created a lot of resentment and then, at one point, it stopped completely. When nobody at the meeting came up with any accusation, the abbot of the time is said to have asked "are you all perfect then?"'

All of which makes it clear that life in Gethsemani has become markedly less harsh. The same is true of other Trappist monasteries. Where once, as one veteran who had been a monk for 60 years put it, there had been 'nothing personal and friendly, now there is a reasonable use of speech and friendly exchange.'

In any case, said Father Carlos, silence could have a negative as well as a positive side for the brothers. 'It can actually be detrimental for someone who doesn't know how to relate to other people. It could be an excuse for not talking to anyone. If you are not careful, your relationships can become very superficial.'

'You can use it to hide yourself away when you should be caring for your brothers. For example, suppose one of them has a duty in the dining room but then gets blamed for not doing something else. You should obviously speak up for him. No, silence can be a professional hazard.'

He had been a missionary in his native Philippines until becoming a monk 25 years ago, and for him the value of silence was that 'it helps me get in touch with a God who is not the product of my mind, the God we have learnt about in our studies. The Holy Spirit has accompanied me in the garden of my identity, He has made me face things I didn't want to face.'

'Every garden has an area of weeds. The Holy Spirit tells us that together we can take out the weeds, the things we don't like about ourselves. That is why, in silence, I seek that voice.' But, I said, there were Catholics who spoke not of listening to the Holy Spirit but of seeking to go beyond all thought in silence. 'That's only because they want to be chic', retorted Father Carlos crisply.

The Holy Spirit did not usually communicate with him in what he called 'physical words' but through a gentle touch at times of loneliness or sadness.

'I was once in a struggle,' he said, 'wondering if I was in the right place. I prayed and prayed but no answer came. So I said to God "why don't you answer, I'm coming to you voluntarily and yet you don't speak!"'

'Then I suddenly realised that God had been speaking to me all the time because, when He is silent, He is asserting himself, He is saying "I am God, I decide when I talk to you, I don't do it on your terms, I do it on my terms. Even in my silence you can become strong."'

'At other times, I have had very clear thoughts which came in the form of words. When I had the so-called vocation to be a monk, I spent five months in a Trappist monastery in the Philippines but felt that it was not for me. So I decided to apply to go to Rome to study psycho-spirituality with the aim of becoming a clinical psychiatrist who could help monks and nuns in difficulty.

'I'd been told that I would be accepted and I was filling out the application forms, spelling out my curriculum vitae with all my accomplishments. Then, suddenly, the voice came: "Do you love me more than these?" So I opened the drawer of my desk, put the forms in there and stopped applying. I sacrificed a whole career, and the German professor who had been encouraging me to go to Rome gave me a hard time.'

'So then I said, "OK but what next?", assuming that a life of silence was not for me. Then the voice came again: "The Philippines is not the only place where there are monasteries." What, I thought, am I supposed to leave my country and my family, all my emotional supports?'

'My colleagues made it clear that they wouldn't help me to leave and then there was the whole business of getting a visa from the American Embassy. That usually took a year at least. My visa came in two days! Unbelievable ...'

He'd also heard the voice speaking in language which suggested that God had a sense of humour. 'One day I was praying in silence and feeling a very deep sense of loneliness. I asked God whether I could live entirely on faith for my whole life. There was no answer.'

'Then came a knock on the door and a man saying, "Father, there is a group of people, Filipinos, who want to see you." "But," I said, "they don't have an appointment." "But, Father, they are Filipinos!"' So I went out to meet them, we had a wonderful time, a picnic and so on.

'When I came back here, I said "Was that you, Lord?" and I seemed to see a smile on someone's face. So I said "could you not do that more often to help me?" And then the thought came very clearly "Don't push your luck, kid!." Now people come all the time.'

Such messages, supposedly from on high and which Father Carlos believes are the Holy Spirit tapping him on the wrist, are often referred to as 'interior locutions' by Catholic and Anglican monks and nuns. It is a rather pompous phrase which they use as code for the inner voice which they believe is the Holy Spirit.

The indirectness, the evasiveness of the way they use the words indicates just how difficult it is to describe the experience. Locution, after all, implies words spoken out loud and, since the words they are talking about are only heard within them, it is not speech as we would normally understand it.

Those who have had such experiences say that, none the less, the words they hear are infinitely more definite and authoritative than the promptings of conscience, that the words do not in any sense come from themselves but from elsewhere and that, although the voice which conveys them is soundless, it is still as if someone has spoken to them – and with a force which is not easily denied. None of those I have spoken to imagines that such locutions make them in any way special, still less that they are thereby elevated in some notional spiritual hierarchy.

One might think that 'professional' religious would be only too ready to claim that they hear that voice very often, if only to suggest a closeness to God, but, if the monks and nuns I have talked to are in any way typical, the opposite is the case.

Some say that they have heard a voice with those qualities only once or twice in lives during which they have spent decades in a monastery or convent; while others, no less devout, declare that they have never heard anything which could properly be described as a locution. In any event, it is one of the most fascinating and logically inexplicable experiences to which Christians can lay claim.

Locutions or not, the monks at Gethsemani are fighting their own spiritual battles, whatever those who come to seek their help may presume. Father Damian was abbot of the monastery for eight years, until he was 75 in 2008, but feels that his education really began at that point.

He is a formidable, powerfully-built man with close-cropped iron-grey hair, and does not find it easy to talk about himself. 'With me,' he admitted, 'there's a certain screen. We all adopt a posture and mine is intended to ward people off.' As we spoke, he seemed to lay aside the screen.

He had not, he confessed, enjoyed being abbot. 'It's a pain,' he said. 'It reveals everything about you. For one thing, it changes your relationship with your fellow-monks for ever. Once you've been at the top, you'll never be equal again. The relationships I have with some of the brothers are different than they were. And then I wonder how many I hurt during my years doing that job.'

It sounded as if he felt, at some profound level, cut off irremediably from the other monks. He wondered, he went on, how Father Carlos could be so open. Carlos just loved people and knew how to entertain them. Why, he seemed to be asking himself – and me – could he not be the same?

As a boy, the son of poor Polish-Irish parents, he had had to defend himself against the other kids, and he'd now realised that he'd grown up with a defensive attitude to the world. 'Then, in the fourth grade, I got a crush on a girl, a nun spotted it and humiliated me, first in front of the class and then in front of the whole school – and I felt there must be something wrong about girls. As a result, I had a very awkward relationship with women.'

Then, after many years at Gethsemani, he had once taken a young monk who needed help to therapy, and had eventually decided to give it a try himself. The therapist had given him an exercise where he was asked to relive his experience at school. A picture came to his mind of 'some kid running through a field laughing, and it was me'.

He had realised that what had happened at school was not his fault but the nun's, and he became free of a hang-up he had had all his life. He was by then 70 years old. Father Damian's eyes were wet with tears as he told me the story.

After he had ceased to be abbot, he said, a new phase had begun in his spiritual life. 'It was as if God had been waiting for all the busyness to be over, so that He could really talk to me. I hadn't imagined my emptiness. He had to tell me how poor I was – which was a great gift. When you know how needy you are, then He's ready to do something with you, when there's nothing covered up any more.'

God had begun speaking to him in a new way. 'When the thoughts come from Him and they come frequently now, they bring a deeper reality because He knows you best. "Oh my gosh," I think, "I should have known that!" It's something new He's doing with me. I don't know if He's getting me ready to go, but I know it's Him. He keeps on opening up His heart, telling me "this is who I am." He's talking about Himself now, He's not talking about me any more.'

'That's why it's important to be silent, and why it takes a lot of silence to discover who you really are and who He is. I wouldn't have arrived at the stage I'm at if I hadn't had so much silence. These things only started to happen to me three years ago – that's why I always talk about a process to those who come on retreat.'

No conversation I had while writing this book was more precious to me than those moments with Father Damian.

6

A chance to hear yourself

Psychotherapists sometimes speak of silence as reverently, as gratefully as any monk.

'For me', said Hymie Wise, 'silence is the most important thing in psychotherapy. In every session with a patient, whether it's with an individual or a couple, silence is the background to everything. All that is said comes from silence and returns to silence. Once you are aware of that fact, you realise that silence is a presence.'

To Wise, who was a Jesuit priest for eight years before he became a therapist, silence is 'wonderfully humble, it never interferes, never interrupts, never makes promises. You can't see it, touch it, taste it, smell it and yet it's greater than all the things which you can taste and smell. My task is just to be present in the silence.'

Other therapists illustrate the value of silence in ways that are both more pointed and more prosaic. Philip Hodson, who has been a practitioner for 35 years, simply remained silent and looked at me, smiling, when I asked him how important silence was in psychotherapy. Ten, fifteen seconds went by and still he said nothing.

'I need words', I said, puzzled. 'You see,' he said with a laugh, 'I was just showing you what the power of silence is like. You felt you had to speak, didn't you? All the detective sergeants in the CID know about that power.'

That is one way in which therapists' encounters with their patients are totally different from visits to a doctor or dentist, where silence plays little or no part, except of the enforced variety. Those who go to a therapist take with them not a virus, back pain or toothache but the tangled web of their lives – their anxieties, confusions, complexes, buried traumas, failing marriages.

Nor do they usually expect the therapist to prescribe pills or potions to alleviate their distress. In these encounters, there are only words and the silences between the words; and any amelioration of their distress can only come from whatever insight, wisdom and inspiration patient and therapist between them can summon up. The experience of therapists suggests that the inspiration is as likely to come from the silences as from the words.

That fact, the complex issues they are trying to address and, in some cases, an innate modesty, mean that reputable psychotherapists are not apt to speak of themselves as if they were a *deus ex machina* or, indeed, anything like it.

'The best therapists', said Robin Daniels, who has been a practitioner for 35 years and is also the biographer of both Yehudi Menuhin and Neville Cardus, 'go into their encounters with patients with a sense of mutual learning. It is *not* top-down.'

Wise goes even further. 'My prayer', he said, 'is that *I* won't help anyone today. If *I* help someone, it changes the relationship between us. Then I'm the helper and they are someone to be helped. That can be a big illusion.'

'When I'm helping you, I'm the strong one, you're the weak one. That's dangerous because at that point my ego begins to appear. So I run away from the distinction between the helper and the helped.'

Which sounds fine in theory, I thought to myself, but how do you maintain that degree of detachment and humility when a patient is so obviously coming to you for help?

For most people, going to a therapist is something of a last resort. For one thing, it seems like an admission that they can no longer cope with life under their own steam. Those who take that step also realise that it will involve delving deep inside themselves, laying bare in some measure the secrets of their lives, not something they would normally choose to do.

They may also suspect that, while there could be a good deal of talk, some part of these encounters will take place in a rather challenging silence, to which most of them have previously been strangers – and that they may find that experience thoroughly uncomfortable.

'People are reluctant to come into therapy', said Daniels, 'because it is a quiet, somewhat silent space. They have an instinct that their conscience is holding regret and shame, and they know that that will have to come out.'

They know, moreover, that any relief from their ills is not going to be achieved in a hurry, that there are no quick fixes in therapy, that they are likely to be seeing the therapist for months, if not years. 'It could take a year and a half to produce anything worthwhile,' said Daniels, 'and if a reconstruction of someone's childhood is involved,

I may be seeing a patient for six or seven years.' For many people, that would not be an alluring prospect.

In his experience, Daniels went on, patients often took quite a while to make up their minds to see a therapist. After another patient had recommended him, there would often be quite a gap before he got a telephone call and then another gap before the patient actually fixed a date.

That was entirely natural. 'The psyche', he said, 'needs time to prepare itself for big events. In that time, a patient's unconscious will be beginning to gather some of the key hurts and hopes which may come out later in therapy.'

The only consolation is that encounters with a therapist are likely to take place not in the cramped confines of a doctor's surgery or a confessional stall, but in the relatively comfortable ambience of a sitting room, with an armchair or couch ready to receive them.

Even so, patients are stepping into what, for them, is strange and unknown territory. 'They don't know what to expect', said Philip Hodson. 'There's a lot of nervous talk to begin with. They'll sometimes say "do I have to lie down?" The medical model is symptoms, diagnosis, cure. Ours is "how can we relate to each other?"'

Patients often arrived early for their first session, said Daniels, and that in itself suggested either a certain nervousness or, possibly, hope. They'd come in looking very serious, trying to absorb everything – the room with all its books and so on – and they'd be asking themselves whether they could trust him.

'What they're doing', he said, 'is tapping into their survival mechanism. After all, it's more than likely that this is the first time they'll have revealed these things, and they want to make quite sure that messages from their antennae are being properly heeded.'

'The first session', he went on, 'often opens with a puzzled, quizzical silence. After all, it's such a different encounter from anything they've been used to. It's so intimate and yet so professional.'

'I'll be waiting for the patient to say what's on their mind but I don't want the silence to become too oppressive so, after three or four minutes, I'll say "feel quite free to sit quietly until you're ready. It may be hard for you to know where to start, but you could just offer anything that comes to your mind."'

Daniels is trying to convey a sense of benign openness but, in that first session, he tells patients quite frankly that, if their meetings are going to produce really valuable results, it will require enormous emotional stamina on their part. Despite that caveat, by the end of the first session they are usually feeling more at ease – and say so.

Thereafter, he recommends that patients frame each encounter with a period of silence, taking 15 minutes or so by themselves before they come into the room to ponder on what they would like to talk about and then another 15 minutes afterwards to reflect on all that they have shared.

Psychotherapists are well aware that, at the outset, a good many of their patients may have no idea how to cope with the silences that naturally occur. 'The current culture', said Daniels, 'is a flight from silence. People are on the run, they fill every spare moment, they can't stand being quiet.'

'I see that mainly as a flight from our dark side, our secret side, our shame. We are also in flight from the unused, under-expressed parts of ourselves. If only people can face the dark things, there's a lot of light behind them. One of the positive aspects of silence is that it can release both imagination and hope.'

'I say to the patients who come, "I want you to have the courage to go into the jungle of your own self. Do that and you may well come out into the sunlight." A therapist can often spot very early on the potential that is waiting to be developed. Even if the topsoil is not of the best, a few inches below the surface there may be some very good soil indeed.'

A key part of that process, in his view, is to try to change the attitude so many of his patients have towards silence. He wants them to discover that, far from being something to flee from, it can actually be very productive. He wants them to become as comfortable with it as two people who are so fond of each other that they are happy to sit together without saying anything.

'For one thing,' he said, 'silence fosters a two-way connection between the left and right hemispheres of the brain. The left side is the one that the Western mind is mostly locked into – the linear, analytical, thinking side. The right side is spatial, creative, intuitive, much wider. In silence, these two sides are more joined up, so you're fully united with your whole self. Not only that, in the process you become much closer to other people.'

'That can lead to all kinds of new insights – such as realising that a pattern of self-limiting or even destructive behaviour is clearly rooted in patients modelling themselves on their parents or other authority figures. I reassure them that I'm perfectly comfortable with being in silence, and that if they can gradually develop a more benign understanding of it, they'll get far more out of their sessions.'

Philip Hodson, too, is trying to reintroduce the benefits of silence to people who have lost all sense of its value. 'In the hurly-burly of *doing*, all the frenetic activity, we don't do much reflecting and listening, we find it difficult to switch off to see what is really happening in our lives. It's as if we were running ourselves like companies, but never doing an audit.'

'Silence gives you a much better chance of hearing yourself, of being in touch with both your conscience and your demons, the voices of discontent and revenge within.'

'In therapy, silence is not like a third person, it's more like a bubble between you. You are both in the silence, but using it in different ways. It is the silence that connects you, you share it and you both contribute to it. Silence is a healing and a loving thing.'

It does not always seem like that: silences can be hostile as well as benign. 'Silences can be healing but by no means always', said Patrick Casement, one of our most distinguished analysts, who was in regular practise for 40 years. 'I went into therapy myself for the first time after a spell in a mental hospital where I tried to commit suicide.'

'The hospital then referred me to their therapist, who happened to be a woman. She was one of those people who made a ritual of insisting that the patient should be the first to speak. For three whole sessions she said not a single thing, and I felt I wasn't going to speak to someone who wouldn't speak to me.'

'Afterwards I drank the best part of a bottle of gin, turned up for the next session, passed out and had to be hospitalised. The next day she actually spoke. She said "what was it you were trying to say with that?" I replied that it had been a complete waste of time for her to be sitting there but not relating to me in any way. What I had been saying was that something had to change! She discharged me and there was no follow-up.' My sympathies are entirely with Casement.

So there are many kinds of silence, and one of a therapist's most important skills is to be able to read what exactly is going on during the silences of a particular session.

'You need to listen for the colour, the tone, the shade of the silence', said Daniels. 'You have to be able to sense just what sort of silence it is. It could be a waiting silence, when the patient is waiting until they are ready for something to come out. Or it could be an absorbing silence, where the patient has shared something deep and is digesting it.

'Or it could be a defended silence, when there is something urgent which *ought* to come out but where the patient is too ashamed or embarrassed to speak of it and so is keeping tight-lipped. Their facial and bodily expressions help you to gauge which it is.'

'Silences are so different', agreed Casement. 'Some patients are silent because they can't put into words what is in their mind, and I don't think a patient has to start with words. The silence itself can be a communication. As you get to know a patient, you begin to sense what is in the room.'

'Some patients use silence as a way of indicating that they don't feel ready to move into words. There was one woman patient who started each session lying on the couch with her fingers straight together, arched like this, and then after five or ten minutes her finger ends would relax. At which point, I would say "Mmm?" and she would speak. In that case, I was letting her silence speak to me.'

'Another person may be on the couch, restless and tense, and in that case I'd try and read their body posture and maybe say, "I get a sense that you are struggling with something today', or "there seems to be a lot of anxiety in the room at the moment."'

'I wouldn't say where that anxiety was coming from. I'd listen to what their state is doing to me and my body. If I felt a mounting sense of anxiety in myself, I'd ask myself whether it was just me or whether I might be picking up something from the patient. If it was me, then I'd keep quiet.'

'Sometimes things come up from them in the silence, but I don't assume that's going to happen. We need to read the silence each time for what might be around. I believe in listening, so to speak, with two hands; on the one hand, it might be this, on the other hand, it could be that.'

In Hodson's view, it is absolutely crucial how a therapist deals with the silences. 'He has', he said, 'to get the pauses right.' Shades of Artur Schnabel, I thought. In other words, he has to play the silence as sensitively as he would if it were a musical instrument.

How long, for example, should a silence be allowed to continue, given that a therapist does not want either to pre-empt the chance of something important being revealed or to turn the encounter in the wrong direction by some clumsy intervention?

'The therapist', said Daniels, 'always needs to watch who is breaking the silence. It should mostly be the patient. On the other hand, there can be silences which are almost punishing. You may want the patient to break it, but if it goes on for half an hour it becomes too heavy. Then the therapist can break it in a very neutral way by asking something like "is that chair comfortable?"'

'There have been times', one therapist told me, 'when I have spent a whole hour in silence with a patient, but only because I could sense them using that time to absorb all that we had talked about previously.'

To Hodson, though, maintaining silence for that long is simply a 'misuse of trade. The longest I've ever gone is four or five minutes and that is a very long time. In that case, I thought I knew the reason for the patient's silence but, in the end, I intervened because there was a chance that I was the problem.'

He could think of any number of cases, said Hodson, where silence had been the key to helping a patient. There had been one man who had had an alcoholic mother and, as a child, had been forced to spend long periods of time with her. 'He told me that he'd often been sitting on a sofa next to his drunken mother in front of the fire. He remembered feeling rigid with anxiety – he was only five years old at the time.

'He wasn't afraid of being shouted at or hit, although those things had happened. What had made him fearful was that this parent was out of control, and he had felt his job was to make sure that she didn't come to any harm. It was a complete reversal of roles, the child had become the parent, you had a five-year-old baby-sitting a 38-year-old.'

'Anyway, one day, the mother fell into the fire and was burned to death. The man told me this story and it took a long time to get it told, with many silences. He kept saying "that poor, poor woman!" There was a long and pregnant silence while I absorbed all this and then four words came into my mind – "but what about you?"'

'He said nothing for a very long time, and that was the crux of the therapy. Up to that point, he had never felt able to think what that tragedy had done to his own life because of his sense of duty as a son, and with such a horrific exit. The silence brought it all home to him.

' "But what about me, what about me?", he kept saying. In the silence, it had occurred to him that it wasn't actually his fault at all. Before, it had always been "oh my God, I should have saved her!" He made a connection he wouldn't have made if I'd been talking. The narrative was told in a different way in the silence and there was a different outcome.'

Through silence, Hodson went on, people made connections which had not occurred to them before. 'There was a lady of 80 who came to me because she was depressed. As it turned out, she had been sexually abused when she was only four, but had never told anyone. She said she thought that that couldn't have anything to do with her life now.'

'I used the silence which followed to get her to listen to what she had just said. After a long pause, she said "d'you mean? … d'you think?" She'd diagnosed herself for the first time. She'd previously been to a doctor who'd asked if anything bad had happened to her in the previous three years. He should have said 76 years. There is no timetable to the human heart.'

In another case, silence had been markedly important, but in a very different way. A couple from North London had come to him with a marriage which had deteriorated so seriously that the husband was sleeping in their car, parked outside. All they did was fight and they had come to him in despair.

'A blind man could have seen what was wrong', said Hodson. 'When the husband spoke, his wife spoke at the same time, and vice-versa. After a while, I clapped my hands together and said "silence! We're going to have a rule here. The only person who can talk is the one holding this pen. Now, let's toss a coin to see who goes first. I'll give the pen to the one who calls correctly and then you've got five minutes each to say what you want." '

'The husband won, so he started – and, as usual, she interrupted. She'd become so sensitive that she felt she had to put up a defence immediately. I shut her up. He had his turn, which actually only lasted for 90 seconds. "Is that it?" I said. "Yes', he replied, with a great heave of his shoulders."

' "My turn now," the wife said, but I told her she'd got to do one other thing first – "tell me in your own words what your husband has just said to you. Can you do that?" She did, though not terribly well. Then she asked again if it was her turn. "Not yet', I said. I turned to the man and asked him whether he would agree that that *was* what he had said. "Pretty much," he replied.'

'Hallelujah', I said, 'you've just had a communication!' '

'Then it was her turn and she went off like an express train. He wanted to interrupt but I stopped him. That couple didn't come back. He stopped sleeping in the car, and they started using car keys instead of a pen to make the other person shut up. In that case, I actually had to impose silence!'

Hymie Wise has spent a significant part of his years as a therapist trying to be alongside couples whose marriages were falling apart. They may already have talked a great deal about the surface irritations that made them despair of the relationship before they came to him. His task, he feels, is to get to the root of that despair. When dealing with a couple, each of whom might have a great deal to say for themselves, the silences were often all the more fruitful.

'I listen to their story', he said, 'and then wonder about it with them in the silence. I ask how they got to know each other and how they came to get married in the first place. They were, let's say, both at the same school and surrounded by friends. He might have thought to himself 'gosh, she's very attractive and gregarious, while I'm the silent type. I'd like to have that gregariousness'. She might have thought 'I'm a bit flipsy, I'd like to have his steadiness'.

'She's all bubbly, he's all solid state. They marry, thinking they'll complement each other. Time goes by and he begins to think "I can't have a serious conversation with this woman, she's a crashing bore." She thinks "gosh, he's stolid, cold, uncharming." They've come to the conclusion that intimacy is impossible.'

Then it was a question of getting them to look again at what they expected of their relationship. 'Wittgenstein is my favourite philosopher,' Wise went on, 'and he said that the body is the best image of the soul so, as I'm sitting with them there in the silence, I try to see what their bodies are telling me.

'Some people live in their heads, some are heart-felt, very emotive, and some live in their bellies. They may be very strong, very stubborn, dug in, but they are often not able to be in touch with their feelings.'

'Now, with the sort of couple I'm talking about, when the proverbial hits the fan, he goes up into his head, she down into her heart. And then they are like ships which pass in the night. He'll look for reasons why they are not getting on and say to himself, "she's hysterical, she just doesn't concentrate." She'll be saying "he's so remote, how can you talk to someone who can't feel?" So they face an abyss where both of them feel alone. They have both become convinced that there is no one there.'

The therapist then needed to call the couple back into the silence and try to find out what it was that had made them think and feel in that way. 'He might say "my father encouraged me to do well in school, and he had great pride in my prowess on the football field."'

'Her story might be "we were told as girls that we didn't need to go to university," so she felt second-class. She doesn't feel accepted for what she is. There is trauma in all that, landmines in all directions.'

'So here we are in the silence,' said Wise, 'and you have to begin to name the beast. I might say to the husband, "I notice that, when you meet a problem, you go up into your head and leave all the emotions behind". To the wife, "you flood the world with your heart. If you could only realise that behind that flood is the fear of being wiped out. When you hear him preaching from his higher viewpoint, you fear for the intimacy of your relationship." The couple then have the chance to reflect on that in the silence.'

Wise guesses that 30 per cent of the couples he has dealt with over the years conclude that they have made a terrible mistake and break up, but 70 per cent – having identified the root causes of their problems – decide to stay together and work on the relationship.

Sometimes, marriages are at risk because of profound traumas that have been locked away in silence and remain unhealed. 'I don't think in terms of words or silence,' said Patrick Casement, 'because a lot is beyond words, even though words are used.'

'A woman came to me who had had five years of what she called gynaecological pain and, for all that time, she'd felt that sexual intercourse was impossible for her. She was in her 30s, so that was causing great stress in her marriage and there was a serious risk of the couple splitting up. She'd previously seen every specialist under the sun and only came to me as a last resort.'

'She was a woman who had gone steady with her husband, they'd married, bought a house and furnished it ready for the arrival of children. The first time she conceived, she'd had a perfect birth but, after six months, the baby – a boy – started screaming and it went on screaming until it died before it was one year old.

'Then the experience was repeated. She had another perfect birth – a daughter, this time – but at six months the baby started screaming, and, just as before, it went on screaming until it, too, died before it was a year old.

'There was a genetic chance that it had happened for the same reasons, so the woman got herself sterilised. By that time, however, she had become pregnant again – so she had two dead babies and a dead foetus. She told me all this with a deadpan face. No feeling was expressed.'

'I was almost in tears listening to it all, but I felt absolutely sure that there were feelings that she couldn't allow herself to be in touch with. I knew I could help her.'

'I said, "I feel you may not have been able to cry about these deaths." She replied that, since the death of the first child, she had never been able to cry. After attending the funeral of her son, she had felt tearful but had "held it in." I said "I feel sure I can help you but it could be very painful."'

'So I led her through the whole experience and, gradually, she felt able to join up with her distress. And then did she cry! I don't want to describe it or try to. The experience itself was beyond words and the crying was indescribable. As she began to be able to bear the emotional pain, it didn't have to be felt in her body, so the gynaecological pain eased. What she had been putting into the gynaecological space was unexpressed distress.'

Was that kind of experience not utterly exhausting for him, though? 'If I hadn't had a dawning sense of understanding,' replied Casement, 'it would have been draining, but this was, in fact, exhilarating because I felt we were getting somewhere. In the end, she was able to enter into a period of mourning which had been so long delayed. It then became possible for full intercourse to be resumed, and with pleasure.'

Those who go to a psychotherapist are buying space and time. Silence and all it can reveal is part of that space. That same silence is also a priceless asset for the therapist.

'On my wall as a child', said Hymie Wise, 'there was a picture of an owl sitting on a branch, eyes closed. It looked at me every night before I went to sleep.

'Underneath, it said:

'A wise old owl liv'd in an oak,
The more he saw, the less he spoke,
The less he spoke, the more he heard,
Why can't we be like that old bird?'

That burnt itself into my soul.'

7

Silences which speak

Had there ever, I wondered, been a longer or more moving silence in any theatre? It came at the end of a play called *Home* by David Storey, which my wife and I saw in the early 1970s.

The play is set in a mental institution and consists entirely of the desultory conversations between the inmates, two of whom are raucous, vulgar women. It is, however, the two principal male characters, Harry and Jack, who engage our sympathies because they are plainly hanging onto the tatters of their identities, desperately proclaiming the respectability of their former lives, trying to keep all kinds of unpleasant truths at bay. The dialogue is spasmodic, shot through with humour, but profoundly poignant.

At the end of the play, Harry and Jack – played by John Gielgud and Ralph Richardson – came forward onto the apron of the stage and gazed out across the audience. The words had trailed away, they said nothing. Harry was already weeping and Jack, too, was soon wiping his eyes.

As they stood there, there was a silence more intense than any I have known in a theatre – and it went on for what seemed like minutes. Their sadness engulfed us all. There were those who wept

with them. It came as something of a relief when the lights slowly
faded with the two men still standing there.

Nobody in the audience moved or uttered a sound, gripped as we
all were by the pathos of their lives. Their silence was more powerful
than any words.

That silence was, in a sense, the culmination of a conversation that
had been going on between the actors and the audience throughout
the evening. It is a conversation that takes place whenever an
audience goes to a theatre to see a play, listen to a musical or be
entertained by a singer or comedian. As any performer will tell you,
playing the silences is as important as playing the words, because
both are part of that conversation. Ralph Richardson used to say that
'the most precious things in speech are pauses', and that acting lay in
those pauses.

'In the theatre,' said Penelope Wilton, who has been on the stage
for over 40 years and, most recently, appeared in the television series
Downton Abbey, 'the audience is half the evening. You're communicating with them the whole time, in silence as well as words, and they
pick up on everything.'

'For example, if I just pushed my hair back like this, they'd think
"what's the matter with her?" There are messages, millions of them,
going back and forth all the time.'

'And I'm listening to them, I never stop, I always have one ear out.
If there's a faint cough in the top corner of the balcony in the largest
theatre you can think of, I hear it though I don't react to it.'

That conversation with an audience, she went on, did not always
require words. 'I once saw a play called *Claybourne Park* at the Royal
Court, and in one scene a man is sitting there eating an ice cream

in complete silence. What you got from him was that he was very depressed, although nothing was actually said.'

'As it turns out, something terrible had happened to his son in Korea. The actors know that but the audience doesn't yet. That's something they'll find out, but his mood previsions something awful, without any words being said.'

Then she'd once done a scene in a play with a young girl. 'The girl was missing her mother and remembering her childhood and I was trying to shake her out of her sadness. "Would you like to draw?" the character I was playing says. "No," the girl replies, "I'm absolutely sick of drawing!" '

'There's then a silence when my character is thinking to herself "what can I do to make this girl feel better?" The audience could read into my thought process – "what the hell do I do here?" They could see that I was lost for ideas, and that was shown not by words but by silence.'

'An actor has to take an audience with him in the journey he's travelling in his head. Silence is a very important part of letting them into that journey. The silences allow them to come with you, think with you, be with you.'

Very much the same sort of thing happened with comedians, she went on. When Jack Benny appeared at the London Palladium, he could walk onto the stage and say not a word. Then he'd look across the audience and, without him having said anything, the waves of laughter would sweep across the theatre.

He'd stop in the middle of some gag. For example, he'd say that he'd been attacked by a mugger with a gun who'd said 'Your money or your life!' There'd then be a very long pause – which gave the audience the chance to think whatever they wanted to think – and then, when he felt the moment was right, he'd say 'I'm still thinking about it'. The longer the pause, the more the audience laughed. 'Silence', said Wilton, 'is fantastically important.'

In theatre of all kinds, it is the audience's chance to become more profoundly immersed in a performance, to relish its humour, savour its nuances, reflect on its meaning, be moved by its pathos – to share in all kinds of ways in the drama.

'It's like a counterweight in a performance', said April Pierrot, a Canadian who has taught at the Royal Academy of Dramatic Art for 20 years. 'There is a huge amount of meaning in silences properly performed. They are where the audience enters most deeply into a performer's thought and feeling. If that reflection, that reaction on their part is not going on, then the performance must be at a pretty superficial level.'

'The actor's processes, which are an amalgam of thought, feeling and action, are what an audience needs to be welcomed into – and, if silence is a natural part of that process, then the audience will be led into that too. If one of those elements, and silence in particular, is missing, then an audience won't be able to respond at the deepest level.'

'The silences, after all, tell you an enormous amount about a character. These days, in a lot of drama, what is on view is just personality, it's all ego and big emotions and, there, silence is less important, but the best drama is making it clear all the time what is going on under the surface.'

'As an audience, we want to see the real things beneath, and, to achieve that, performers must allow the silences to speak for themselves. If they're just thinking in terms of personality, then they're not likely to make a good actor.'

That said, the use of silence in a theatre also carries enormous risks. As with speech, timing is all. 'If you are going to achieve a meaningful silence in a Shakespeare play,' said Tim Pigott-Smith, who has been an actor for over 40 years, 'it needs to be worked for by everyone on the stage. It interrupts the language and can be very potent providing you're taking the audience with you.'

'If, on the other hand, it's not been agreed on by the actors, the audience won't know how long it's going to last, and the silence will be a real mess. So silence is a danger. Conversely, if you can work towards a silence and the audience knows what's going on, it can be very powerful. The murder of Julius Caesar, for example, can be done without anyone saying anything and then it intensifies the focus wonderfully.'

'I remember a marvellous moment in the Ian Holm and Estelle Kohler *Romeo and Juliet*. Ian is very tiny and the balcony is very high, so he stood on a wall and she lay on the balcony floor. She put her hand down and he just managed to touch her fingers.'

'That was an unforgettably wonderful moment after all the words that had been spoken. It was a concentration, a synthesis, a focus, it summed up everything that had gone before.'

'So silence is a very powerful tool in the theatre and, if it is properly used, it can be more powerful than anything else. In purely technical terms, it's also a way of stilling a restless audience.'

'If you try and speak more loudly to compensate for coughing or restlessness, you'll fail every time. If, on the other hand, you take your level right down, they really have to listen – and, if you just stop in the middle of a sentence, they'll become conscious of the noise they're making and it'll refocus things on you. That's something you can only do by instinct.'

'I used to enjoy making a big noise as a young actor but it just didn't work. While he was doing King Lear, Ian McKellen said to me, "I shan't be happy until I've done every line as quietly as I possibly can.'

'In this little play I'm in at the moment – *Educating Rita* – I have to take my jacket off at the end of a scene as Rita leaves the stage. Then, rather than have a blackout and the energy of the play be dissipated, we have a half-lit stage and I move off to collect a desk.'

'The audience is focused because they know that that's how I'm going to teach Rita. So the whole thing is in complete silence, but that silence is quite intense because we're keeping the energy of the play going and the audience is watching like mad.'

The trainee actors and actresses who go to RADA spend their three years there learning how to use silence as well as their voices. 'The issue of silence is always on the table', said Willi Richards, who has been teaching there for 19 years, 'because actors are trading in silence as much as in speech. From the moment a curtain goes up, they have to be attuned to silence as well as words, so we spend a lot of time getting them to learn how to do nothing and say nothing while they're on stage.'

'Of course, we teach them acting techniques,' said Tom Wakeley, a vocal coach at RADA, 'but the ability to be open to an audience is partly God-given. That's one reason why we ask our students to perform before an audience of teachers and other people from the college before they go out and perform in public.'

'That's often when something remarkable happens, the God-given thing you cannot teach. You can tell a student to listen to the audience and how to use silence, but you can't say "take so many seconds," because it's a matter of feel. Don't forget, it is the most terrifying thing for an actor to stand on a stage and do and say nothing. On the other hand, if they do it well, it's riveting.'

If an actor was going to be able to produce magical performances, said April Pierrot, they also had to develop an *inner* silence while they were on stage. 'There are all the clichés about the fact that silence in drama is absolutely essential. We tell them, "you must let the material speak for itself, you must listen to the other actors, you must be in the right state to perform", and so on, but doing all that properly comes from an actor being able to give himself over to an inner silence – dwelling within the text in a very silent way. It's exactly the same for a musician.

'To achieve that, the body and the feelings have to be married to the intellect. If actors are only using their minds, they won't be in that inner silence. It is very difficult to be physical, mental and emotional at the same time, but you need a marrying of all those elements to create a great performance.

'It's that inner silence which enables an actor to both listen to an audience and, at the same time, be present in a performance. Then they're rapt, absorbed – and that quality of raptness in a performer is something that transmits itself to an audience, if they're receptive and perceptive. They're absorbed, immersed just as the performers are.' That raptness, that complete absorption, is what we experienced when we saw Gielgud and Richardson in *Home*.

There are no stage directions for silence in Shakespeare, though the silences are there, plainly demanded by the action and waiting to be exploited in all kinds of ways by a sensitive director.

When Cordelia is asked what she can say to improve on her sisters' protestations of love for their father, she replies 'Nothing', and when Lear retorts 'Nothing can come of nothing', the silence is ominous and full of foreboding. Hamlet's soliloquy 'To be or not to be' has, perforce, to be full of hesitations, pauses and silences since he is thinking of taking his own life.

In *The Winter's Tale*, Leontes' wife Hermione is wrongly accused of infidelity and sent to jail. Her husband eventually learns that his suspicions were quite unjustified but assumes that, after 16 years, she must have died. So, when she reappears in the form of what seems at first to be a marble statue but then turns into a living woman, Leontes is struck dumb and Hermione at first says nothing. Given a good director, the silence that follows can be deeply moving, with Leontes plainly riven by guilt for what he has done.

Over the last century or so, silence has become an ever more prominent feature of the dramatist's art. Directors are no longer left to decide where silences would be appropriate. Playwrights often specify them in the text and, in the case of Samuel Beckett and Harold Pinter, the pauses and silences are, as Pinter's biographer the distinguished theatre critic Michael Billington puts it, 'meticulously orchestrated'.

In *One for the Road*, Pinter calls for no less than 18 pauses in the space of four pages, and in one page of *The Caretaker* there are seven pauses and two silences. He even varies the number of dots between words to indicate the length of a pause, almost like a musician writing a score.

'Sometimes there are two dots, sometimes three,' said Billington, 'and there is a legendary story of Pinter watching a rehearsal of one of his plays and saying "I think you're giving me a two-dot pause when I've asked for a three-dot." For him, a pause meant a brief, dysfunctional hesitation, whereas a silence implied a change of mood or emotion.

'He believed that words alone cannot convey meaning and that it is silence which can express those things which are beyond words. He even wrote a play called *Silence*.'

Billington once asked Pinter when he had first discovered the power of the pause. Pinter replied that it was going to the London Palladium in the late 1940s to see Jack Benny perform. After watching the way in which Benny played the audience with pauses and silences to lead up to the punch-line of a joke, making them more pent-up with expectation all the time, he had realised what he could do with the pause in his own plays.

In the years when he had been an actor himself, he had also been influenced by working alongside Sir Donald Wolfit, the magniloquent actor-manager of the post-war years. He had once seen Wolfit, in Sophocles'' *Oedipus Rex*, turn away from the audience with a cloak outstretched and observed the dramatic power of that silent gesture.

'For Pinter,' said Billington, 'the use of silence is also a canny deployment of an actor's resources and it is often, particularly in his later plays, a way of establishing the gravity of a situation.'

'He uses it for comic effect too. Take, for example, *The Caretaker*, where the three men are living in a ghastly flat filled with rubbish, there's a leak in the roof and they're all looking at the leak and watching the water drip from it. The water drips, the laughs build and the silences get longer!'

Reading the actual script reveals the masterly way in which Pinter exploits both drips and silences.

A drip sounds in the bucket

Mick – 'You still got that leak?'

Aston – 'Yes.' *Pause* 'I'll have to tar it over'

Mick – 'You're going to tar it over?'

Aston – 'Yes'

Mick – 'What?'

Aston – 'The cracks'

 Pause

Mick – 'You'll be tarring over the cracks on the roof?'

Aston – 'Yes'

 Pause

Mick – 'Think that'll do it?'

Aston – 'It'll do for the time being'

Mick – 'Uh!'

Davies (abruptly) – 'What do you do …?'

 They both look at him

 'What do you do … when that bucket's full?'

 Pause

Aston – 'Empty it'

The laughs come off the page even when one is not in the theatre.

Pinter also uses silence to produce dramatic tension. In *Old Times*, silences carry a threat of uncomfortable revelations as the characters recall their past lives. What, the audience wonder, is going to come out next after there has been another silence?

He even uses silence to create a sense of menace of a very different kind. 'In *Old Times*,' said Tim Pigott-Smith, 'Deely is sparring verbally with a visitor who sees him as a competitor and he asks her if she would like another drink.'

'I used to collect a bottle of water from the waitress and move towards the woman with the bottle. You could play with the ambiguity. I half-smiled but the audience didn't know whether I was going to pour a drink or hit her with the bottle. It's the most menacing thing I've ever done on a stage.'

Pinter was by no means the only playwright to deploy silence in an entirely new way. Samuel Beckett was another who believed that it could be just as expressive as speech. *Waiting for Godot*, first performed in 1955, has four characters, but silence becomes like a fifth. There are as many as six directions for silence on one page, and the play only works if it is full of expressive silences.

Beckett also wrote a play called *Breath*, which is the theatrical equivalent of John Cage's 4' 33". Although there is no text, Beckett said ironically that 'it is written in English'. The curtain opens onto a stage littered with rubbish, the 'action' consists of 30 seconds of silence, interrupted by two 'faint, brief' cries and the sound of breathing, which Beckett directed should be amplified. It is the nearest thing we have to a play that takes place without words and in almost total silence. Needless to say, it was not a box-office hit.

This deliberate orchestration of silence, says Billington, is essentially a twentieth-century phenomenon and he regards Chekhov as 'the first genius who realised that a play must contain the three elements of speech, silence and sound effects to create the symphonic realism of which silence is such an essential part.'

The ending of Chekhov's masterpiece *The Cherry Orchard*, first performed in 1904, is a perfect illustration of that symphonic realism. Madame Ranevsky and her family have had to sell their beautiful country estate, the windows are shuttered and they are leaving to catch the train for Moscow. There is the sound of the doors being locked and of the carriages driving away. Then there is silence and, in the stillness, there is the sound of an axe chopping down the beautiful cherry trees.

Unfortunately, the family have not realised that they have left Firs, their 87-year-old retainer, locked in the empty house. The last thing we see is Firs bemoaning the fact that he has been totally forgotten. 'Ech!', he says, 'I'm good for nothing', and lies down.

Then, in the silence, a sound is heard that seems to come from the sky. It is like a breaking harp-string and it dies away mournfully. Everything is quiet again, and nothing is heard but the strokes of the axe far away in the orchard. 'The sound of the harp-string breaking', said Billington, 'implies that society's bonds are broken too, that change is inescapable, that revolution is coming. No words are spoken, but it is one of the most powerful endings in modern drama.'

What was it, though, that caused playwrights such as Beckett and Pinter to staunch the torrent of words that had been deluging English stages for over 300 years, and espouse the use of silence in such a revolutionary way?

'One of the reasons', said Billington, 'is that, at some point, twentieth-century dramatists became suspicious of language, speech and words with their capacity for hypocrisy and obfuscation. Pinter was always attacking politicians for their distortion of language. The rediscovery of silence is tied in with the way public language was being misused.'

'The second thing is that a good deal of modern drama is about waiting. *Waiting for Godot* is really about human life as a process of waiting, and there were other plays in the 1950s which were about the boredom of existence.'

'The old certainties of religion and politics no longer existed and these were plays which expressed a sense of life's meaninglessness. As waiting became a dramatic symbol, there was an increasing exploitation of silence.'

'Another reason why silence became more important in twentieth-century drama was an increasing minimalism in art of all kinds. You can see it in painting, music and the theatre. Artists were trying to discover how much you could do without, and silence became a more important component when there was this search for the absolute minimum.'

'There is a whole school of theatre at the moment which is anti-text and anti-language. The avant-garde believes that theatre has been drowning in words. The phrase "text-based theatre" is pejorative so far as they are concerned. They want to escape the verbal weight of the past. They're much keener on thoughts, emotions, the use of the body and silence.'

'Of course the glory of English drama is words, but there is a new generation which wants to jettison all that and go back to the roots of theatre in silence and mime. And it's perfectly true that, if you are overtaken by the power of silence in a play, you identify so strongly with the action of the drama that words become inadequate.'

Penelope Wilton has acted in a number of plays by both Pinter and Beckett and experienced their dramatic impact. 'Beckett wrote a play called *Krapp's Last Tape*', she said, 'in which, for the first ten minutes, there are no words spoken at all. He opens a drawer, takes out two bananas and eats them in complete silence. Then he takes out some tapes and plays them. It's a man reviewing his life. He only says three or four things and the play lasts for an hour and a quarter.

'There's another of Beckett's plays which is called *Eh Joe* and, in it, there is a voice which speaks to Joe. I once played the voice. We find Joe sitting on a bed. He looks under the bed, shuts the door, gazes out of the window, shuts the curtains and looks in the drawer at the bottom of his wardrobe.'

'Then he sits down on the bed and this voice from nowhere starts to take him through his life and all the women he's treated terribly. It keeps saying "d'you remember that one, Joe?" '

'That really is minimalist', I said, implying that I had not really missed much by not having seen the play. 'Yes it is,' she replied, 'but the repercussions are enormous. They can reveal a man's whole life.'

As our contemporary world has exploded with sound, much of it vulgar and fatuous, so some of our dramatists have had recourse to meaningful silences.

That finds an echo in the people who train our actors. 'Silence is a crucial form of communication', said Willi Richards. 'It may even be fundamental. We have this egocentric idea that only our utterances have value and that silence is only useful because it gives value to those utterances, but the silence may be the more important thing.'

8

Opting for the quiet life

There cannot be many universities in the world where there is absolutely no one to be found at eight in the morning. I was visiting the Maharishi University of Management in Fairfield, Iowa, and had stupidly locked myself out of my room. I walked up and down the road hoping to find someone who could help me. There was nobody to be seen.

As a last resort, I rang the emergency help line in the lobby of the Maharishi Men's Peace Palace, where I was staying – there is a Women's Peace Palace right next door – but all that offered was a message telling me where I was, something I fortunately knew already.

Eventually, it dawned on me. The 1,300 students and staff of this, the principal American centre for that curious and fascinating phenomenon Transcendental Meditation, were presumably all meditating, either collectively in the two golden domes down the road or in the privacy of their own rooms. Just as in other TM centres I had visited, breakfast did not start until nine. For those who practise the TM form of meditation in a serious way, the previous two hours are sacrosanct.

At last I found a security man – not a practitioner of TM – who kindly drove me into Fairfield, a pleasant two-horse town that also proved to be surprisingly quiet at that time, perhaps because a sizeable proportion of the population also practise TM. For lack of any obvious alternative, I consoled myself with a blueberry muffin and a cup of tea from a gas station.

Amazing, really, that an institution based on the ideas of an Indian holy man, Maharishi (literally, great seer) Mahesh Yogi, should find itself in a remote little town in the Midwest; and even more amazing, that an American university should be based, as this one is, on silence, the last thing one expects in the United States, that carnival of wall-to-wall, 24/7 words and music.

Silence really does matter in this university. All the students have to complete a Development of Consciousness course which involves a considerable amount of meditation – and they cannot move on to the next semester unless they have fulfilled its requirements to the satisfaction of the university authorities.

'You have to take part in at least 70 group meditations in each semester', a Kenyan who is doing a Ph.D in Management Studies told me, 'plus a residence course that lasts for two days. Then there's a meeting each semester for all the students, where meditation is discussed and people share their personal experience.'

'Each time you meditate, you have to swipe your identity card to show that you've been to the meditating group. If you've not been often enough, you get an e-mail pointing that out to you. And then, just to make sure that you're getting all that you should out of your meditation, you're checked twice every semester by certified TM teachers.'

So that, I thought, was why there was a notice outside one of the rooms at the Maharishi Men's Peace Palace which read 'Personal Checks of TM Technique in Progress'. To my astonishment, I discovered that, at the end of every morning class, there is an obligatory period of meditation, which lasts for ten minutes.

Maharishi, the instigator of all that is happening on the Fairfield campus, first began teaching TM in the United States and Britain in the 1950s. For his British devotees, the moment of his arrival there – 13 December 1959 – is a red-letter day, the beginning of a new life for them. He came proclaiming large ambitions – creating world peace, no less – but proposed a very simple spiritual practise: to meditate for 20 minutes twice a day.

His message did not carry any obvious religious content, it was not a philosophy or belief system, and it did not involve reflecting upon one's own moral and spiritual condition. 'Considering one's life is no part of the TM process', said Richard Johnson, TM's national director in England. The old, rocky road of confession and repentance was not on the agenda.

What TM did promise was that, as your internal noises were quietened in silence, you would experience a fourth state of consciousness beyond sleeping, dreaming and waking; and that having achieved that state, you would become aware of your deepest and best self. That moment of 'transcendence', TM promised, would be blissful and help people to discover an ease and stability that would allow them to flourish in every aspect of their lives.

'When you practise TM,' said Anne-Marie Wilson, a TM teacher in Oxford, 'you automatically settle down and achieve a very deep level of rest, measurably twice as deep as deep sleep.'

All this made a considerable appeal to a generation that was turned off by organised religion. It offered an escape from the stress and cacophony of their lives. It seemed to be both discipline- and guilt-lite, it carried a whiff of Eastern promise, and it did not seem to be asking too much of them.

'The majority in this country', said Charles Cunningham, one of TM's English publicists, 'don't do TM for spiritual reasons. They do it to help them cope with their busy lives – to feel calmer, more in control, to sleep better, to become more emotionally robust.'

TM's impact became all the greater after celebrities such as the Beatles climbed aboard the Maharishi's bandwagon. Courses by newly-qualified TM teachers became available, often at a fairly modest cost. Those who signed up were given a mantra – a 'sacred' word to act as a focus for concentration – chosen by their teacher from a range of 30 to fit his (or her) reading of their character and needs. They had to promise not to divulge their mantra to anyone else.

There is no doubt that TM provided a lifeline for many, at all kinds of levels. Anne-Marie Wilson, who could hardly bear to speak to her mother, got on much better with her after she had started meditating. Barry Spidach, who learned to meditate while he was at Oxford, 'slept better and laughed a lot more!'

Carole Branson, then a headmistress at a primary school in Hertfordshire, had felt 'ground down, unhappy and tired' after marrying, in 1975, a husband who she says had a problem with alcohol. She then came across TM, went along to listen to a talk, met 'nicely-spoken men in suits' and decided that she would rather spend £40 on learning to meditate than on buying clothes which would soon be out of fashion anyway. Without TM, she said, she might not have survived.

Stephen Warren, a retired chartered accountant, met TM in 1975, when he was 28 and 'going through a very stressful time. There had been too many changes at work all at once, I was starting to have a couple of sherries when I arrived home and I had begun to be afraid that I might be heading for a nervous breakdown by the time I was 40.

'Then I saw a TM poster claiming that it offered relief from psychosomatic symptoms and I thought "that's what I've got." When I went along to meet them, I'd expected an Indian guru talking a lot of oriental gobbledygook, but what I found was a suave young man in a suit. I took to him right away.'

'After I'd learned just a little about TM, I had the most beautiful sleep of my life and it started to release a whole heap of tensions. I began doing the 20 minutes twice a day and had another beautiful sleep. By the Monday morning, I was a different person at work. Instead of snapping at anybody who interrupted my thought processes, I found myself saying "good morning, how are you?" It did me a power of good.' It sounds like a version of being born again but without any of the usual religious baggage.

For those who found their 20-minute meditations fruitful but wanted to go deeper, Maharishi came up with an altogether more demanding form of practise in 1975. There is certainly nothing discipline-lite about the TM-Sidhi programme, as I discovered when I spent a night at Carole Branson's B & B in Rendlesham, Suffolk.

I arrived a little after five o'clock but found that she was not there to welcome me because she was doing her early evening practise in a meditation room dedicated to the purpose, and could not be disturbed. Sidhas, it turned out, meditate for up to two hours twice every day, morning and evening, and observe those hours with unswerving regularity.

So, having been asked by Richard Johnson, who was there to make the introductions, if I would mind taking off my shoes – another feature of TM life that mimics an Eastern habit – I was shown into the most spotlessly clean bedroom I have ever seen. If I were to find my way to heaven, I imagine the sleeping quarters would be something like that, possibly minus the laughing photograph of the Maharishi that I found gazing at me amid the glowing whiteness.

When Carole finally emerged, she was reluctant to say too much about what she had been doing during the previous two hours, for fear of making other TM-ers feel that they were doing their practise in the wrong way. It did, though, she said, involve breathing exercises, yoga postures, the repetition of sutras – Sanskrit sayings from the Vedas which, again, you never revealed to anyone else – and yogic flying.

Flying, I said? Yes, said Carole, at a certain point, when you were at a very deep level inside, you repeated a particular sutra and it happened – your body left the ground.

Some would say, she added, that you could only fly if you had been sitting in the lotus position, but there was no way she could achieve that given her age – 59 – and weight. She had certainly never expected to fly but, in the split second after she had repeated the sutra, her body had moved upwards.

Nothing unusual about that, said Johnson. All sidhas expected to do it. You sat on a foam mattress and, at a certain point in the

TM-Sidhi programme, in a moment of transcendence, you experienced 'a sort of impulse' and your body rose spontaneously and without the least effort. Nor did you just hop around, there was some evidence of people remaining in the air for more than a brief moment.

The experience was blissful – a favourite TM word – but it was not a selfish exercise, said Johnson. You were doing it for others, because when enough people flew together, it 'dissolved negativity in the whole environment and created a wave of positivity'. In one way, that is not so very different from the benefits which monasteries and convents, and, indeed, any faith group hope to confer on communities which live close to them. Virtue may be its own reward, but others may also be inspired by it.

That, Johnson went on, was why sidhas throughout Britain synchronised their flying activities. The agreed flying hours – which, I am tempted to say, don't require air traffic control – are eight in the morning and six in the evening. If all of this sounds too preposterous for words, it is worth reminding ourselves that there are Christian doctrines which sound equally fanciful to non-believers. Even so …

Silence, said Carole, was where it all came from. The 60 houses on the little TM estate in Rendlesham where she lives are all designed as 'houses of silence' according to the principles of vedic architecture.

Each of them has a brahmastan – a still centre – which brings a shaft of light down through the house from a sort of cupola on the roof to a glass panel in the sitting room floor. 'That', said John Renwick, who designed the houses, 'is their silent core.' It all pointed heavenwards, added Carole piously.

Each of the houses faces eastwards, which, she said, meant that 'we'll get the support of nature.' The Maharishi, indeed, had declared that any TM-er who lived in a house that did not face east should get out of it as if it were on fire. All their entrances were either on the east or north, the master bedroom is above the meditation room and all waste is flushed to the south.

It began to make one feel as if TM-ers are being given a head start in the spiritual life: they certainly think so. 'This', said Carole, 'is a loving, supportive house which helps me to be the kind of person I want to be. I have never had a house before which loves me as this one does. It's a support for silence and, without being too New Age about it, it's a loving silence, like a guiding hand that points you in the right direction.'

Interestingly, both Carole and Richard were raised as Catholics. There had, she recalled, been quite a long period when she had wondered whether TM was OK, but she had come to realise that it was and that, indeed, it had helped her to understand her faith better.

Richard, for his part, now goes to Mass only occasionally and the impression I had meeting TM practitioners in both Britain and the United States is that their TM practise has, in many cases, largely taken the place of any religion they had before. A good many of their original beliefs none the less remain: Carole, for example, still believes in transubstantiation – the conviction that the bread and wine become the body and blood of Christ during the Eucharist.

There was certainly no shortage of faith among those who set up the TM colony in Skelmersdale, Lancashire, in the 1980s. The aim of those who flocked to that unlikely spot was to prove the validity of one of Maharishi's most cherished – and, many might think, wholly implausible – theories: that if the square root of one per cent of any community meditated (and presumably flew) together, that community would be radically transformed. Economic activity would burgeon, crime rates go down. So, when 75 empty council houses became available in Skelmersdale, convinced TM-ers from all over England took the plunge and headed north. For some, it was an extraordinarily sacrificial act of faith.

'This is, for the most part, an enclave of the South.' said Bill Stevens, a former TM teacher from London, 'and we came here purely so that we could meditate together twice a day. When people meditate alone, it's like dropping a pebble into a pond, it creates ripples that go out into the collective consciousness. When a lot of people meditate together, it's like throwing in a rock. That creates waves, the impact of which can be measured.'

At the outset, the aim was to gather 800 meditators in the little Lancashire town. Sadly for TM, they never achieved anything like that number. Still, when their Golden Dome was opened in 1988, there were enough for Richard Johnson to feel able to claim that, as a result of their collective efforts, the crime rate in Liverpool – the nearest conurbation – had come down against the trend and, indeed, remained lower than it might have been for the next five years. That, however, was the last hurrah.

The TM community now numbers only 180 and, although their faith and practise remain high, what they have been able to achieve is modest compared with their original aim.

Each morning and evening, the faithful – the vast majority of whom are over 50 – appear at the Dome to meditate, men and women separately, and a good number of them value their hours in silence so highly that they embark on programmes which require them to meditate for even longer.

When I met her, Annie Mercer, an Oxford graduate and the wife of the part-time director of the community, was involved in a curiously-named programme called The Invincible Assembly. She was spending no less than nine hours every day at the Dome and was doing it for a fortnight.

Yet, despite all the dedication, TM is not flourishing as it once did. Stevens reckons that there are between 50 and 100 qualified TM teachers in the Skelmersdale community, but that only a handful of them still teach. Having himself taught for 20 years, he gave up some time ago – 'I just got fed up with being broke' – and is now a senior executive in the construction industry.

'There are perhaps ten people learning TM each month in Skelmersdale,' agreed Titus Mercer, 'whereas we have the capacity to teach 1,000. There's just not enough demand locally.'

In America, by contrast, TM seems to have found something of a second wind. I took the brief ride from Fairfield, Iowa, to the somewhat grandly-named Vedic City, whose 260 houses are all designed according to Maharishi principles, to meet Dr John Hagelin, TM's chief administrator in the United States. He was once known as *raja* but prefers a more American-sounding title.

A physicist who came to TM via Harvard, Cern and Stanford, he is a large, confident-looking man snugly dressed in a roll-neck sweater and jacket.

TM, he said, was experiencing a wonderful renaissance in the United States. In the last two and a half years, since he took over, there had been a seven-fold increase in the numbers learning TM in

America, up from a few hundreds a month to a couple of thousand. Three hundred and fifty public schools had incorporated TM in their programmes. Applications for the university were going up by 50 per cent every year.

So, why was this happening? 'It's mostly my looks', replied Hagelin with a faint smile. No, one of the main reasons was that TM's scientific research was so much better than it had been. For example, a nine-year study conducted at the Medical College of Wisconsin had shown that the practise of TM reduced heart attacks and strokes by 47 per cent.

Then, the American Medical Association, which had no interest in TM, had been 'wildly positive' about its effectiveness in the reduction of diabetes as a condition. They had put out 'a really extraordinary press release'. TM, said Hagelin, needed to do that sort of research because we were living in a scientific age and, for a pill to be presented and sold, it required evidence of its effectiveness. The facts showed that TM was cheaper and a lot more effective than drugs.

Maharishi, he went on, had been the first to publicise meditation in the West in the post-war years and, at the time of the Beatles, TM had been It. Then other people had tried to hang onto its coat-tails and a cesspool – no, hodge-podge – of other meditation techniques became available.

So people needed to be told where to turn and the research pointed them in the direction of TM. TM, he implied, was not just any old meditation. It was 'evidence-based meditation.'

The other reason why things were looking up was that TM was now much more customer-centred. Maharishi, who had died in 2008, had been 'a great charismatic force' and he had talked a lot about world peace – but that was not going to inspire more than one in a hundred Americans to meditate. They were far more interested in reduced blood pressure and making sure their children got better grades in school.

So, yes, TM would still help world peace, but it would also lead to lower blood pressure and less strokes, and it would help your child with its ADHD (attention deficit hyperactive disorder) problem. TM had 'the world's greatest meditation product', and they were now presenting it in language that people could understand.

In other words, Hagelin is intent on playing down the lofty, windy aims of the founder and, instead, emphasising the more concrete perceived benefits of TM – all of them in line with the intense American preoccupation with health.

TM's foot-soldiers could not agree more. They needed the research, said Barry Spidach, since many people thought TM was 'flaky' and they required proof. 'We are not snake-oil salesmen,' declared Ken Chalkin, one of TM's American publicists, 'because we have the research to back up what we are saying.'

What the Buddha and the Christian saints who spent their whole lives in silent contemplation would have made of all this one can only imagine. To them, meditation was certainly not a product, but we are in America and, in America as elsewhere, products need endorsement. That is why TM has turned to research to try to revive its fortunes. Hagelin is convinced that, within two or three years, its operation in Britain will experience the same renaissance.

To its credit, far from evading scientific investigation, TM actually promotes it. Since 1970, over 600 studies have been published in 130 journals. All of them seem to indicate that regular meditation improves life in all manner of ways: 38 per cent better concentration levels in children with ADHD, improved maths scores and athletics performance, lower crime rates, the alleviation of depression ... the claims fly at you like grapeshot.

Hagelin is only too ready to add a few of his own. 'Meditate twice a day', he said, 'and the IQ goes up, even in the elderly. With TM, intelligence and creativity can develop right through life.' Whereas students typically became a little less intelligent during each of their four years in college, given the practise of TM you could document an *increase* in their IQ levels year after year. Could Harvard, he wanted to know, claim the same for its students? The message seemed to be that TM works. Silent meditation can never have had more voluble proponents.

There is one of Maharishi's notions that TM has not abandoned: the transforming effect on a community, or country, when the square root of one per cent of a population meditate and fly together. When 400 yogic flyers converged on a town in Southern Holland in 2006, one of TM's publications claims, the result was that the economy grew twice as fast as it had in 2005, the stock market rose dramatically, crime and accident rates went down.

The same sort of thing had happened in the United States, the book maintains, when the Invincible America Assembly opened in Fairfield in 2006. By July of the following year, the stock market had risen by 27 per cent.

The belief that such dramatic 'results' are possible has made TM determined to build up a permanent group of 2,500 yogic flyers in the Fairfield area. To that end, they have invited advanced TM practitioners from all over the country to stay on or near the campus, and pay them up to $830 a month to help them with their living expenses.

Even more startling, they have imported from India around 1,000 vedic pandits – young men who have been trained by gurus since childhood and have spent their teenage years in ashrams. 'Since the square root of one per cent of the US population is roughly 2,000,' said Jefferson Aikens, who helps look after the Indians, 'we needed a professional group to beef up the numbers.'

The pandits come for two or three years and live on a separate, fenced-off campus in low, white buildings that, from a distance, look like a rather smart army camp. They are all, needless to say, yogic flyers – they have their own flying hall – and they fly at the same times as the TM-ers in the golden domes.

'They are very happy', said Bhupendra Dave, their Indian supervisor. 'They play cricket and do a couple of trips a year, but for the most part they lead an enclosed life. It is like a two- or three-year retreat. We have 40 Indian cooks to look after their food and the cooking is better than it is in India.'

'It is like taking a piece of India and dropping it into the middle of the United States', said Bob Wynne, the mayor of Vedic City who doubles as the *raja* of TM's operations in New Zealand, Kenya, Armenia and Pakistan.

The result, Wynne went on, was that they now had 2,000 people meditating and flying each day, morning and evening. It seemed churlish to observe that they have not yet produced any particularly beneficial effect on the American economy.

There is no doubt that, over the years, TM has helped a good many people to a greater or lesser degree, and is still doing so. It would be hard to imagine a more relaxed and amenable bunch of people than the ones you meet in Fairfield.

The students, in particular, clearly love the friendly atmosphere of the university and a sizeable proportion value meditation enough to sign up for the TM-Sidhi programme.

'It's so different from the university in Syracuse where I was before', said Graham Torpey, whom I met in the Annapurna Dining Commons, the oddly-named dining room. 'There, the point was to work your socks off and then make your first million by the time you were 24. Here, it's about the development of the self, and silence is the golden building block at the heart of everything.' Was it, though, worth the $32,000 a year in tuition fees? 'It's worth ten times that', he replied.

No one in the world talks about the value of silence in a more articulate and appreciative way than TM-ers. They speak of it as an ocean of untapped potential in which all of us can discover a new calm and creativity.

To the outside observer, though, it seems a pity that they should then go on to make claims which seem, at the very least, grandiose and, to all save its most ardent devotees, preposterous.

9

Letting go

On Easter day, there were two Americas on show in Albuquerque. In the morning, thousands attended a sunrise Mass. In the evening, a constant stream of cars crawled along the city's main street, windows open, music blaring, full of half-naked men in what looked like bondage gear and, on the sidewalks, more-than-half-naked women. 'They like to cruise on Sunday nights to meet people for their intimate encounters', said the hotel clerk drily.

This is the city where Father Richard Rohr, Franciscan friar and a celebrated global guru of the Christian variety, has his base. It is a modest establishment on the south-western fringes of the city, a low building with a simple porch. In the entrance hall, a tiny fountain plays.

Welcomed into the garden beyond, visitors can sit in the shade of a 125-year-old cottonwood tree while bees investigate the clover. Here, there are none of the ornate trappings of institutional religion, no odours of sanctity. In a country in thrall to speed and noise, this is an unpretentious oasis where time is the servant, not the master, and silence the default setting.

Rohr himself turns out to be as unimposing, as outwardly unclerical, as the place. He comes into the room wearing a bomber jacket and a baseball cap. He is accompanied by his dog, a Labrador called Venus. He is of medium height, balding and with a rather sparse grey beard. His complexion tends towards the rubicund. He could, you think, be a retired pharmacist.

It is the eyes that set him apart from the ordinary – shrewd, sparkling, perceptive. He made me think just a little of Mahatma Gandhi, another unimposing, understated figure who spoke quietly but had great purposes.

Gandhi, of course, gave his life to set a nation free. Rohr is trying to persuade a nation which is already free to reach out and claim a different kind of liberty, to throw off not colonial oppression but the suffocating shackles of self.

Rohr founded the oddly-named Center for Action and Contemplation (you might think it should be the other way round) in 1986. 'It was set up', said a young woman who helps to keep the grounds tidy, 'to inspire social activists who always seemed to be *against* something. Richard wanted them to be *for* something, to operate in a way that was grounded in justice and peace, but behave with real humility.' In other words, Rohr did not want to blunt their passion, simply to purify it.

In this, as in so many other ways, he is totally unlike the popular stereotype of the American evangelist. His personality and manner of life are the antithesis of glitz and showbiz, of glib and well-rehearsed answers.

For the last dozen or so years, when not travelling, he has lived in a little hermitage about a mile from the Center. He told his Franciscan superior that, if he was going to be able 'to go deeper' as well as standing in front of crowds as 'some sort of guru', he would need 'big chunks of silence and solitude'.

He tries to spend four or five of his waking hours alone, writing, gardening and house-cleaning, but always going about with 'a listening ear', practising silence.

He admits that he often does not succeed. 'I start worrying about problems, thinking in the wrong way about an upset with a staff member – and I can spot myself doing it. I say to myself "you're obsessing about that, making your case in your mind." I did it today. I was supposed to be silent, but in fact I was rehearsing a future conversation.' How refreshing, I think, to meet a fallible guru.

Nor does Rohr present the usual picture of doctrinal rectitude, ticking all the standard boxes of belief. He is catholic in his attitudes as well as Catholic in belief. I asked what he thought was the best religion and, with a breadth of mind worthy of the Dalai Lama, he replied 'whatever religion leads you to an experience of God. If Christianity does not lead you to a *de facto* union with Him but Hinduism does, then that is the truest religion for you.'

At the same time, he is quite ready to fire a shot across the bows of brethren of a different persuasion. 'Protestants worry me', he said. 'They're so tied to words that they have no way into their right brain. Endless sermons, arguing about words …' But then, he added self-deprecatingly, Franciscans didn't have a strong moralistic tradition, they were always thought of as lightweight, non-doctrinaire.

Oddly, perhaps, for a man who believes so profoundly in silence, he has written 25 books that have achieved a remarkable, world-wide readership. Amazon bought 60,000 of the latest, *Falling Upward*, pre-publication. Rohr's spiritually acute, non-doctrinaire mind-set clearly appeals to a great many people.

What, then, of silence and its value? He was not sure, said Rohr, that you could have an experience of being close to God without it. That was how important it was. But the kind of silence he had in mind was not just a matter of excluding 'auditory noise'. It was a silence that was both deep and involved us letting go of a great many things.

If you wanted an effective experience of silence, you had to let go of your own agenda, your attachment to your ego and to the image you had built up of yourself. If there was not that wholehearted detachment, then it would still remain your own agenda. The phrase 'unless you die to yourself' could, he said, perhaps be better rendered as 'unless you renounce yourself'.

Of course it was the small self, the false self that he was talking about, the self that we had built up to cope with the challenges of the world, because people needed to know who they were in terms of roles and titles. They had to construct a significance, an identity for themselves. The trouble was that we all got hooked on that, we took it too seriously.

He knew that it was not an easy matter to lay all that aside because there were big advantages in continuing to be that false self. The world paid and promoted us for being that way. It did not want us to become the self God had always had in mind, for the simple reason that it could no longer manipulate that self. How, asked Rohr rhetorically, could you manipulate a Mother Teresa?

The other pre-condition for a really fulfilling practise of silence was that we had to be entirely *present* for it. The way in which he used the word implied that it was not just a matter of being in a room and saying nothing for half an hour.

Being present, explained Rohr, meant having your head space open, your heart space open and your body ready and waiting – and the body was important because all too often it held remembered hurts. So *that* kind of presence was what he was talking about, that kind of readiness, that kind of willingness, that kind of vulnerability.

Without that kind of presence, we would always remain in charge, and the silence he was talking about meant, above all else, stopping being in charge. It meant, in other words, being willing to take our hands off the wheel.

Then, he went on, when we stopped being in charge, we connected with a different kind of reality – 'the world as it really is, us as we really are. Looking at people and things with the eyes of God, not with ourselves as the reference point.'

'Silence is the only way to pull us out of that entrapment. We're so used to evaluating ourselves from our own perspective, "what's in it for me?," "do I like this or not?" True silence doesn't evaluate, it simply values, it allows things to be what they are, without us dissecting them all the time.'

'We simply don't realise how much we've substituted the mind for reality. We think our way of thinking about the moment *is* the moment. The philosopher Descartes, brilliant as he was, represents for me the nadir of Western philosophic arrogance with his "I think, therefore I am."'

If we wanted to begin to see things as God might see them, Rohr went on, we had to allow ourselves to enter a silence where our preferences were no longer the point of reference – what or whom we liked or did not like.

People might well ask, I said, just what was the benefit of all this? 'Don't start there', retorted Rohr. 'That is already an appeal to the utilitarian, pragmatic ego – "what do I get out of this?" OK, I obviously hope that you'll get a lot out of it, far more than you can possibly imagine, but the point is to search for a union with the divine.'

'The fruits will be what it talks about in St Paul's letter to the Galatians – love, joy, peace, longsuffering, gentleness, and all the rest. You become a different person. Add to those things the fruit of healing. People spend tens of thousands of dollars going to therapists and I'm not against therapy, but, this way, you will just fall into becoming your true self.'

'You'll have saved yourself all that money and you'll stop going on about "father didn't hug me enough" or "my mother died when I was six" and so on. This way, you'll stop defining yourself by all those hurts, being what is called wound-identified. Because, this way, we worship a man, Jesus, who rejected the idea of being wound-identified. He said, "I am resurrected, I rose again." His body had terrible wounds, but they did not identify him.'

So what would actually come to us in silence? Would it just turn out to be a blank, warm space? There was a debate, I said, between those who argued that we should seek, in silence, to go beyond all thought and those who claimed that God was able to give us clear thoughts, clear guidance about our lives and how we should live them.

He himself, replied Rohr, did not believe that they were entirely contradictory ideas. Most forms of Eastern meditation laid bare our attachment to our own thinking processes.

'But Christian meditation goes further than that', he went on. 'I don't think we need to put as much emphasis on posture or asceticism or even success in the process of meditation as Eastern religions do. Our reliance is on the inner voice speaking for and to us, what we call the indwelling presence of the Holy Spirit.'

'I come down on that side of the debate while thinking that the Eastern forms of meditation have much to teach us. That inner voice is omnipresent, it is inherent grace – and all you can do is get out of the way with your mental fabrications and overlays. If you can do that, you will always hear a deeper voice. Poets sometimes know that better than clerics.'

So, how did that inner voice reveal itself? In silence, could we expect to hear so-called locutions? 'I'd never use the word locutions myself,' said Rohr, 'because that leads you into the left side of the brain. No, it's not hearing words.'

What then about St Paul, when he was thrown off his horse at Kawkab on the road to Damascus? He had asked God what he ought to do and was told to go on into the city. After three days without either food or water, he was then told to go to the street called Straight and to the house of a man called Judas. Those words seem to have been very specific.

Well, replied Rohr, he was not going to deny that God could choose to operate in that way. But, in general, he did not think the inner voice had that kind of audio quality, although some people said it was almost audio, it was so clear and real.

Generally, the inner voice was more likely to come in thoughts and convictions, or in the shape of deep feelings or even dreams. Jung said that, when we had a great dream, we would know that we were being spoken to, and God did speak through dreams.

What had often struck him was that, when people claimed to have received locutions, they always seemed to come in the vocabulary of their own cultures. For example, when he'd heard that a Swiss had decided to go to Guatemala to help provide clean water, that to him showed signs of being the voice of God.

On the other hand, when the three children from the village of Fatima in Portugal said that they had seen souls falling into hell like leaves from the trees, that sounded to him like 1910 Portuguese Catholicism!

You could recognise that inner voice in a number of ways. For one thing, it was always bigger than your culture, your religion. And it always sought for something that stretched you beyond your comfort zone.

We simply could not tell God how He should communicate with us. There were those who said that He did not love gay people or people in a second marriage, and that we should not love them either. Excuse me, no church could decide whom God was able to love! We might want the right to decide who is lovable and who isn't, but if we did that, we had just acquired a labelling mind and, once we did that, we'd killed religion.

'The sickness of America', said Rohr, 'is superficiality – to be showy, spectacular, the richest, the prettiest, all of which is nothing but showmanship. And that lack of depth keeps Americans from reality.'

'When you go to the depth of anything, even evil, there you will meet God. If you stay on the superficial level, you merely *use* God.

Some of the evangelicals make me want to weep, they're so silly, they try to make Jesus into just another consumer product. Silence always leads you to depth and I'm afraid Americans are allergic to silence.'

'My own understanding of the Gospel is that we are meant to be totally involved in the world but seeking God not through doctrinal knowledge or formulas, but through direct experience of Him. And it shouldn't be "the Pope says" or "the Bible says", it should be a movement from exclusive reliance on some outer authority to an increasing trust in our own inner authority.'

'The kind of silence I've been talking about is the door to the big picture and it is spacious enough to hold that big picture. It is not just self-reflection, it's not just ruminating about our thoughts and opinions about things. Opinions, after all, are just thoughts that we've wrapped around ourselves.'

'That's why I put Action first in the title of this organisation, because you don't have anything to contemplate unless you're fully engaged in the world of flesh and blood. Without that, you're just gazing into your own navel.'

No better place to seek the kind of silence Rohr spoke about, I would have thought, than St Benedict's monastery at Snowmass in Colorado. It nestles unobtrusively at the head of a broad, sweeping valley in the Rockies. It does not set out to impose itself on the landscape in any way. It seems to say 'I'd really rather that you didn't notice me'.

The buildings, somewhat drab in appearance, are almost hidden from view behind a dark glade of pine trees. Encircling the monastery high above are the snow-capped peaks of the Elk range, two of which soar to more than 14,000 feet.

The silence in this landscape, which is at once majestic and forbidding, is so intense, so all-pervasive, that one of those who came to stay at the retreat house across the valley had found it so oppressive on his first visit that, when he came back again, he brought with him a machine which created white noise. The receptionist who welcomed me said that his own children quite liked to have the carpet sweeper switched on.

The howling of coyotes can wake visitors in the early morning and there is a notice in the retreat house that offers advice to anyone who happens to come across a black bear on their way to Mass. 'Do not make eye contact', it says. 'Try to look as large as possible by raising your arms and jacket. Do not run, just back away slowly – and keep your fingers crossed. It could be your last retreat.'

I had come to Snowmass to meet Thomas Keating, a Trappist monk who is not as well-known as Merton but has none the less had a great influence on many people's lives around the world. He has written a number of books in which he has sought to harmonise the wisdom he sees in Eastern religions with the contemplative traditions of Christianity. He recommends a method that he calls Centering Prayer.

Walking across the valley through an early spring snowstorm but with fortunately not a black bear in sight, I waited for Keating in the monastery's book store, which makes it obvious that this is a place of breadth as well as depth. There were translations of two well-known Sufi poets, Rumi and Hafiz, and a book entitled *The Amish Way*.

Keating was 88 years old when I arrived and, since I am something of a pessimist, I had been afraid that he might have been called to higher service before I got there. I need not have worried.

He comes in dressed in an all-enveloping habit of some kind. He is large of frame, broad of face and gentle of manner. He did not strike me as being old. He had a quality of quietness and stability that inspired confidence. I sensed that he had travelled in spiritual realms of which I knew little, if anything.

I felt that he might well have things to say which I would find mysterious, but which none the less I very much wanted to hear. And so it proved.

He was mystified and saddened, said Keating, by his own country-men's antipathy to silence. They even went to sleep with earphones on. Silence had been pretty much repressed in both America and Britain, because it was distrusted and feared. In many churches, there were liturgies that left no place for it. That represented the overwhelming of religions by our culture.

And yet silence was part of our nature, an essential aspect of being human. Without it, any kind of human development and maturity was impossible.

That sounded like quite a big claim, even for a man who has given his life to silence. How could he say that, I asked? Keating was clearly astonished by the incomprehension that lay behind my question. 'Because our nature is absolute silence', he replied. After all, where the heck did we come from? Silence. And where were we going to?

No, everything came from silence, including God. Silence was not something you had to go out and get, it was something you *were*. Silence was the house in which we lived but which had no limit, no boundary – there were no doors, no windows, no ceilings or floors.

The words did not tumble out. They came slowly, steadily, thought-fully. Keating was not selling me anything. He was drawing from a deep well of insight and experience. Listening to him, I felt I was in the presence of a large and generous spirit. It was sometimes hard to follow where he was leading but I wanted at least to try.

Silence, he went on, was probably the best way to have a profound experience of God. He had once called it the first language of God. That was just a poetic statement intended to get people's attention. What he had meant was that our own first language is the one we are most comfortable with and so, if we wanted to speak with God, then why not use the language He was most comfortable with, silence?

The reason silence was so important had to do with the Christian belief in the God of three persons, the Trinity of Father, Son and Holy Spirit. It was what Keating called 'a Trinitarian mystery'.

The Father, God, was infinite silence but contained every possibility, all potential. The Son, Jesus, was that potential come to realisation, because the Father had emptied Himself into the Son. You could call that a sacrifice, said Keating, the total gift of oneself. And then the Son emptied Himself back into the Father. He lived in the Father rather than in Himself. And the fruit of that sacrifice was the Holy Spirit.

Years before, I had heard a priest, Anglican as it happens, speak of the Trinity as a three-purpose motor oil. He had no doubt wanted to be helpful, to make the concept more accessible, but I had felt totally repelled by what I regarded as the prosaic, banal nature of the image. The words of Keating, on the other hand, stirred me deeply. I had never heard such a beautiful explanation of the Trinity.

What, I asked, was Keating's own practise of silence? 'I just open myself to it all the day long,' he replied, 'except when I forget! It's not that I know what silence is, but I know that it's there, and that in it

I can find what I truly am, my true self. In doing that, I'm opening myself to a mystery because nobody knows who they really are, they just think they do. We all try to create something of a self, we go about it vigorously from the moment of conception.'

So what exactly was Centering Prayer? The thing that distinguished it from other forms of prayer, said Keating, was that it started out from an attitude of *kenosis*, the Greek word for emptying.

It meant emptying yourself, it was like putting out the garbage. It did not involve talking, nor was it thinking or remembering. It meant listening to the Holy Spirit. That did not put speaking prayers out of business, it just moved prayer onto a more intimate level where it became an exchange, a conversation with God, even – sometimes – a communion with Him.

It was letting God speak to you through the heart, normally without words. It helped you to be attentive and alert to that little nudge of divine guidance, that brief sentence suggesting what you ought to do or say. And if God was telling us what to do, surely doing it would be appropriate? These things would come to us without effort on our part.

We just had to beware, said Keating, that it might not be God speaking, because the false self also made suggestions to us. For example, if you were told to give that guy a punch on the nose, you might reasonably infer that it was not the sort of recommendation the Holy Spirit would give you!

What you tried to do was to integrate the workings of your heart and mind with the intention of obeying the will of God, and with an attitude of humble submission. When he spoke of the heart, said Keating, he was speaking about intuition rather than analysis.

Analysis belonged to the managing mind, which always tended to be talking and thinking about something, whereas the heart spoke without words and without any logical progression. The heart spoke with the deep voice of intuition.

As for the mechanics of Centering Prayer, they were simple enough. He suggested 20 minutes in silence twice a day (which sounded remarkably like TM). He did not think people should do too much or take it too fast. It should be a moderate practise, people should move forward with prudence.

After all, no one knew what they were going to meet in silence and it could be horrendous in the beginning because it put us in touch with the hurts we had suffered in the past. Silence was a very potent thing.

It awoke two things in the unconscious, said Keating – the positive energies of grace and the God who dwelt within us; but it also released the emotional wounds which we had repressed. It could be really traumatic if the things that came up in silence were almost too painful to look at – being unloved, deep emotional wounds, abuse. Some people were afraid of silence for very good reasons, hence his view that it was wise to take it slowly and seek help if you needed it.

Fortunately, however, silence did not tell you 'the whole darn story' all at once. There was a kindness to it. It released all those repressed wounds at a rate we could handle. It prepared you gradually to trust the divine therapist.

There were other attitudes that we needed to develop which went along with the practise of silence. Just as in a conversation with a person, you might have to wait for the answer, an answer that did not depend on you. You should not go away until you had the answer.

Waiting was part of listening and silence enabled you to listen to God's response. Then you were ready to accept an infusion of divine light, life and love, a shorter term for which might be grace.

He would just like to encourage people who tried to practise Centering Prayer to be patient, not to get up and leave the conversation with God. After all, we were not paying for it and it was a very high-value service we were getting from the Ultimate Reality.

The practise of Centering Prayer also involved letting go of the way we usually reacted to major events – people entering and leaving our lives, divorce, the care of the sick, death. You should not just react to those things. You should respond to them in a way that was truly spiritual, accepting things as God's will but always believing in a God who wanted us to do something about the situation.

As you went on with Centering Prayer, it became a kind of spiritual marriage, though it might sometimes require a rather long engagement depending on how much needed to be emptied out first! But, however long the engagement, it infused every other kind of prayer and turned it into a living conversation.

At a certain point, you stopped trying. Why search for something you already had? That did not mean a sheep-like passivity, it was an emptiness which was beginning to be filled with something.

At first you might not be sure what that something was, but soon you would find that what was being opened inside you was a capacity, innate in human nature, to have a boundless confidence in God and a sense of gratitude for all His gifts. That, in turn, released our creativity and we started to manifest God's generosity in our own lives.

Somewhere along the way we would learn more and more of our true self, the unique self that God had made us to be. As that uniqueness was revealed, we gave God and Christ a chance to be part of it – and then we really had something to give back to God.

The day I left Snowmass, spring was struggling to arrive. The birds were singing and the mountain flowers were beginning to open. There was brilliant sunshine on the snow-clad peaks. I found it hard to say goodbye to Thomas Keating, to my mind the very best of America.

10

The silence of the mountains

I went to the Engadin in Switzerland for a holiday, not imagining that my time there would have any part to play in this book. I wanted nothing more than a chance to relax and to relish the pampering which the finest Swiss hotels can provide.

It was there, though, that – much to my surprise – I came to appreciate the kind of silence that I had first encountered, though only briefly, in the Rockies – the silence of the mountains. There, I had felt its intensity but, since that had essentially been a time for talk, had thought little more about it.

In the Engadin, by contrast, there were days – indeed weeks – in which I did little more than walk alone in the mountains. It was then that I had the chance to experience and ponder on the remarkable quality of that silence.

Hermann Hesse, the German novelist and poet, called the Engadin 'paradise on earth', and he was not exaggerating: it is one of the most beautiful places in the world. If you go south-east from St Moritz you enter a land of shining blue lakes beneath snow-capped peaks and,

among them, you will find some of the finest mountain walking in
Europe.

On one morning, in weather which the French call *grand beau*, I
took the cable car at Furtschellas and climbed by way of steepling,
stony paths on to the Wasserweg, a trail which takes you across a
great sweep of rocky outcrops and deep valleys in which are hidden
half-a-dozen Alpine lakes.

It is a vast expanse of silence and stillness and, in the hours that I
spent there, the sounds of modern life never once intruded and the
human presence was negligible. The works and the words of man had
dwindled away as if they never were.

The majesty of the landscape, with the great grey peaks towering
above, has a scale and a timelessness – unchanged for tens of
thousands of years – which puts you firmly in your place, makes
you feel just how small and insignificant you are, how trivial your
concerns.

'Up there,' said Cecile Giavanoli, a guide who has been walking
these mountains for 30 years, 'it doesn't matter who you are, it makes
no difference. People who would like to be important or feel they are
great, they don't – because we're not.'

'In the mountains, you realise how small you are. It's reality, it's the
truth of who we are. If you are thinking up there "I'm so great," you'd
know you were lying about yourself.'

In that majestic context, feeling self-important would, indeed,
be ridiculous. Some may come to the Engadin by helicopter, others
second-class on the train, but, once up there, they are all the same.
The garb of class, like the self-importance, vanishes without effort,
and so too do the masks which we are apt to don to confront the

world. The artifice and the posturing slip away and we come closer to the core of ourselves.

The whole process, together with a sense of physical vulnerability, prompts an inner stillness. The silence, moreover, is so profound, so all-embracing, that it seems to have a presence of its own. You have to pay attention to it, to honour it instead of ignoring it as we usually do. It is the realm through which you are travelling.

This is not the silence of the forest path or the lonely lakeside. This silence is limitless, echoing. The austerity, the grandeur of the landscape only serves to deepen it. The usual diversions are far away. I never saw anyone wearing earphones in the mountains.

Cecile maintains that she is not at all religious, and is not expecting anything particular to come from the silence, but she none the less insists that 'it is certainly not nothing'. What that 'nothing' amounts to she finds it impossible to describe or explain, but she is sure that, in some way, it makes her feel more open, more present, more aware.

'Up there,' she said, 'you just become more sensitive to what is around you. Animals, flowers, your feeling for them is much more intense. That may be because there is no influence from other people or from noise. The backpack of family, relationships, shopping, all the daily duties, chores, routine, have been taken from you. All you need is a map and the right clothing to cope with the weather. Then, if you are quite alone up there, you become closer to your real self.'

There is something both refreshing and relaxing about being in the silence of those high and lonely places. Perhaps because they inspire a sense of awe in the face of the great and unfathomable, an awe towards whatever or whoever created them, simply being there seems to give life a new perspective, to offer the possibility that our lives could be altogether simpler, less driven, less cluttered.

Up there in the silence, the senses are sharper, the mind clearer, the spirit freer. There suddenly seems to be so much mental space in which the mind can soar like a bird, unencumbered, liberated. You feel within yourself an extra potential, not for worldly success of any kind but for a new openness and generosity.

When you have made your way down to the valley again, utterly exhausted, knees not so much aching as trembling, you feel – each time – that something has been released in you. Because of that you feel gratitude for the silence that, quite unbidden, has yielded so much.

Occasionally, though, even in these mountains, that silence can be painfully fractured. One morning I took the cable car from St Moritz up to the Corviglia and began the long walk across the mountain's shoulder towards Silvaplana. The silence was not as absolute as it had been on the Wasserweg – the buildings of the town were still a distant prospect – but it was still quiet enough for me to be absorbed in it.

Then, suddenly, I heard the sound of music, and noticed three loudspeakers, perhaps 15 metres apart and connected by a cable, half-hidden in the long grass at the side of the road. They were broadcasting a Mozart quartet. Now, normally, I would feel nothing but joy to hear the sound of Mozart, almost any Mozart, almost anywhere – but not, please God, not *here*.

I felt assaulted, affronted, angry that someone, for whatever reason, should have seen fit to infringe upon, to pollute the silence in that place. For me it was an act of desecration, of unforgivable and tasteless intrusion. I never did discover who was responsible or what they thought was to be gained by it. All I knew was that I wanted, for once in my life, to leave the sound of Mozart far behind.

I walked on and soon found myself at the foot of the great Suvretta Alp, the scree slopes of which led to a summit garlanded with light summer clouds. Once the silence had been restored, I experienced a sense of profound relief. It felt so soothing, so refreshing.

And I realised, perhaps for the first time, that man-made sound even as beautiful as that of Mozart can never equal the gracefulness of silence in such a place. The painful contrast brought home to me how much I was beginning to appreciate the silence of the mountains.

Near the Waldhaus, the hotel where we were staying in Sils Maria, there are two valleys. One, the Fex, is a tourists' dream. It has hotels, restaurants, horse-drawn carriages for hire, well-marked, wooded paths and a roaring, tumbling torrent of a stream.

It is stunningly beautiful, easily accessible and offers everything needed to satisfy both the inner and the outer man. As a result, its paths are exceedingly well-trodden.

The second valley, the Fedoz, is further to the south and boasts none of these charms. It is modest and retiring. It has no hotels where you may stop for a refreshing drink. The views to the snow-clad peaks at its head are unspectacular, the path up its southern flank much less well marked, because it is clearly not used so often. Many mountain walkers simply pass it by and some regard it as downright boring.

On three or four previous visits to my hotel, I had never once been there. I had walked past its entrance a dozen times, seen nothing in it that seemed of any particular moment and moved on to more spectacular delights.

This time, knowing of my interest in silence, Cecile had suggested that I should go there. So, one day, I took her advice and set off up the path along the Fedoz's flank. As it happened, I felt rather heavy of heart that day, gloomily reflecting on a once-precious friendship that had recently seemed dented beyond repair. There were no visual splendours in the valley to ease my mood. What there was was solitude, a complete absence of human beings and a silence profound enough to wrap me in a peaceful, undemanding nothingness.

From time to time, a swallow flashed by and there was the occasional whistle of a marmot warning its mates of an alien presence. Otherwise, for two whole hours, I saw and heard nothing.

Yet, as I walked up that unspectacular valley, my mood slowly changed. There was no dramatic illumination, no great miracle – why should there be? Somehow, though, in that companionable silence, my heaviness of heart was eased. The sun flashed a smile on my face. I noticed a simple, yellow, orchid-like flower gleaming amid a wilderness of rough grass and rocks and, for some reason, it seemed like a symbol of light and hope.

I felt, in that silence, as if I were in the presence of a sympathetic friend who understood my sadness but passed no judgement on me. A desire came over me to be as open, as receptive, as undemanding and welcoming as that modest and unassuming valley. I realised that the time had come to learn from the past and to let go of it.

I came back down the Fedoz a different person. I did not quite know what had happened, but something had and I was truly grateful. When I go back to the Engadin, I shall not head, first of all, for the sumptuous splendours of the Fex, with its hotels and its rösti-serving restaurants, but for the sparse and silent glories of the Fedoz. In St Moritz, I had noticed an archway leading to some of the shops that makes a candid declaration of intent. 'Happiness is expensive', it declares. In the Fedoz, it comes entirely free.

Silence on the heights of the Engadin is not what it was. Marcella Meier, now in her nineties, remembers when 'everything was done by horses'. Until 1925, cars were simply not allowed. In her mind's eye, she can see 50 two-horse sleighs, their tiny bells jingling, waiting for travellers to arrive at the railway station in St Moritz.

Even so, she says, there are many places, many little valleys where you can still find real silence, the silence that, to her, is 'absolutely necessary for a healthy life'.

In it, she believes, we return to ourselves, we begin to feel a part of the natural world. Of course, she said, it was harder to feel self-important in the mountains if only because you became painfully aware of how feeble you were. The mountains were eternal, they stood there with all their history and all their silence. In that silence, we could find ourselves again. I knew what she meant.

11

A shared silence

I had imagined that Quaker gatherings would be quiet, not to say silent, affairs, but I had scarcely got through the door of the Oxford meeting house before a grey-haired lady bearing a bundle of magazines buttonholed me.

'Can I interest you in buying a copy of *Peace News*?', she asked, in a tone which suggested that purchase was well-nigh obligatory. 'It costs 50p.'

'I'm interested in peace but not the news', I replied, in a vain and rather fatuous attempt to fend her off.

'Yes,' she retorted crisply, 'but are you taking any action about it?'

'As a matter of fact,' I said, 'I'm sleeping quite well at the moment', but even this retreat into whimsy did not deter her. 'Well,' she retorted in the manner of an old-fashioned hospital matron, 'we shall have to find an antidote to that!' Not short of a word or two, these advocates of silence.

The meeting which followed was much more what I had been expecting. The room could hardly have been simpler or plainer. There were benches with cushions, arranged in a square, so that the people who came could sit facing each other. Apart from that, nothing more than a piano and a vase of flowers. To all outward appearance, it could have been a meeting place for the National Secular Society.

The congregation were equally unadorned. There was a scattering of beards, no undue smartness of dress and one red beret among the hundred or so who were there. Most had grey hair but there was a fair number of 20- and 30-somethings. There was none of the social chatter that precedes many an Anglican or Methodist service.

A woman announced, briefly and as if reluctant to break the silence, that this was going to be an all-age service and that, in half an hour, the children would come in to present a Christmas play with carols. That may have accounted for the piano.

Then everyone became quiet again. For half an hour, there was total silence, broken only by the occasional, slightly apologetic cough. It was a thoughtful, reverent silence. Some sat with eyes closed. There was very little movement, an almost complete lack of restlessness. On this occasion, no one spoke, no one got up to 'deliver ministry', as Quakers put it.

What, I wondered, was going on in these people as the minutes ticked gently by? Were they praying, for themselves or others? Were they making petitions to God? Were they contemplating some amendment of life? Or were they simply seeking for divine inspiration?

Tot homines, (or, for the matter, *mulieres*) *tot sententiae*: ask a hundred Quakers and you are likely to get a hundred different responses.

For Stephen Yeo, formerly the principal of Ruskin College, Oxford, the point of the silence is 'to let in, to discover The Other who is not me, to help me find my place in the world'.

It made him think of Lear – 'that silly, vain King desperately seeking love, who finds himself with his Fool on a heath in a storm with no clothes on. He realises his powerlessness and, in that moment, discovers his humanity. That's what I'm looking for in the silence, to find my humanity, to put myself in a larger context, realising that you are infinitely less significant than you would like to be.'

'We're not meditating,' said Deborah Filgate, who went to a Quaker boarding school in America, 'because that would separate you from everybody else, and what we are seeking is a common silence.'

The first thing she always did at the meeting was to try to leave her immediate concerns behind and then go round the room mentally, thinking of each person and their needs. Quakers call that 'holding them in The Light'. There were, she confessed, three ladies she did not get on with and, in those cases, she tried to look for the positive things about them.

'In the silence,' said Ian Flintoff, who played opposite Spike Milligan in all 637 performances of the play *Oblomov* and took the part of Marcellus in the Daniel Day-Lewis/Judi Dench *Hamlet*, 'we're seeking for the Spirit, that part of the human personality which is of God. The silence enables that Spirit to be expressed.'

'I'm definitely not meditating and, as for communicating with God, absolutely not. It's more like a focus, a certain inward repose. For me, the meeting is about the others rather than myself, the people I'm grateful to be with. Some Friends close their eyes, but I never do. I want to be aware of the time and the place and the people I'm with.'

'When I go into a meeting, my mind will be so busy, so full of words', said Margaret Osborne, who attends a Quaker meeting in the West of England. 'There'll be many voices in my head – "I really shouldn't have," "did I remember to do that?" – and I find the silence very healing, calming. It helps put things in perspective, things which have been blown out of proportion because of the hurry of life. It's a cleansing or adjustment process.

'I ask for guidance about how to sort things out. Sometimes I'm moved to tears, trickly tears and then, though I can't say I hear a voice, I'm conscious of a presence within me and I'll get what you might call a noiseless thought. It's in words, though I'm not conscious of any sound of words, and I profoundly believe that it is the voice of my God.'

'For Quakers,' said the oddly-named Ben Pink Dandelion, who is Professor of Quaker Studies at the Woodbrooke Centre in Birmingham, 'silence is to be in the presence of God or the divine or the mystery, it is the realm where we can hear God and get rid of all the stuff which gets in the way. Many Quakers would say they're trying to rise above the internal hubbub.'

He was born Benjamin Stout, but, after becoming an anarchist in the 1980s, decided along with his comrades to change his name as a protest against the fact that your father's name was just passed down to you. He deliberately chose one that was both 'unusual' and ambivalent as to gender. Legally he is still Pink Dandelion but would rather be called Ben.

'The absence of the outward', he went on, 'leads to a greater sense of the presence of the inward. In that inward encounter there is, for me, a tangible feeling of being in The Presence and, if you stay in that place, you will be guided. I talk about having an accompanied life. God is with me at all times, and a lot of Quakers would agree.'

'When I have to take decisions, I'll go into silence and try to discern. I'm trying to live in the world but not be too much part of it. Never monasteries or convents, but a mysticism in the world.'

When Quakers came out of a meeting, said Stephen Yeo, they would often comment on the quality of the silence. They would discuss whether it had been a generative silence or a dull one, and they would often agree even if nothing had been said. They would sometimes also speak of it as having been a 'very gathered' silence, a feeling that they had all seemed to be of one mind.

Nothing, surely, could illustrate better than these testimonies the sheer versatility of silence – that apparent nothingness – to meet the needs of people who turn to it for help and succour. Since, so far as traditional Quakers are concerned, silence is better than speech, they are not expected to break it lightly or ill-advisedly.

If they are moved to say something during a meeting, it should ideally spring from the inspiration of the moment and not from some pre-prepared contribution. What is said should both come out of the silence of the meeting and add to it in some way.

'People talk about "getting a holy nudge", said Ben Pink Dandelion, 'being pushed onto their feet. Typically, they'd speak for two or three minutes and what they've said will be received in total silence as people reflect on it. It's not intended to be part of a dialogue. Nobody is expected to speak more than once. If someone went on for 20 minutes or spoke two or three times, then one of the elders would intervene.'

'I have heard ministry where I've asked myself "what is that?." Someone once got up and said "My video on bereavement is coming out on Thursday, price £14.99," and I thought that's not ministry, that's a notice. But the mention of bereavement led to a string of beautiful contributions, so you never know what's going to move a meeting!'

He had never, he added, known a meeting go wrong 'in a performance sense', but they were always at the mercy of those advertising worthy events and the verbally incontinent.

What Quakers gain from silence is critically important because, liturgically speaking, it is all they have apart from 'ministry'. In Britain and the more traditional parts of the United States, at least, there are no sermons, no collective prayers, no hymns, no incense, no incantations, no baptism, no Communion, no order of service – none of the normal trappings and rituals of Christianity.

It is hard to overstate just how odd all this really is. To begin with, Quakers are the only faith group coming from a Protestant root that gives such primacy to silence. They are the very opposite of the talk-and-sing routine which marks so much of Western religion, where silence has a negligible role. In a part of the world where so many shun silence, here are folk who proclaim that it is one of the keys to a sane and healthy religious life. For that reason alone, they are both a phenomenon and something of a treasure.

Silence offers another, quite uncovenanted blessing to the Quakers. As Ben Pink Dandelion shrewdly observes, 'it tends to mask our diversity because people don't have to share their beliefs. Previously, there was a purely Christian understanding among us but, these days, what Quakers believe can vary very widely.'

Polls suggest that 75 per cent of Quakers believe in God, but there are plenty of outspoken nay-sayers. 'I don't like the word God,' said Deborah Filgate, 'and, so far as Jesus is concerned, there probably was such a historical person, but his importance has been completely overblown. All those direct quotes reported years after he had died! The beginning of the Lord's Prayer, those are I think his actual words, but he's not an important figure for me.'

'I certainly believe in the existence of such a person,' said Ian Flintoff, 'and Jesus did say some inspirational things, but we know more about the X and Y chromosomes to make it credible that he was the Son of God.' Margaret Osborne, too, thought that 'the jury is still out on that'.

'Quakers', Flintoff went on, 'don't sign up to any set of beliefs. In fact there's almost a doctrine of anti-doctrine, and that is very unifying.'

'We have no creed,' agreed Deborah Filgate, 'and I've been to a meeting where you had an agnostic at one end and a very Christian person at the other and it made no difference whatsoever.' She had known someone push what she called 'the Christian thing', but that was very rare.

Having once had a very firm belief system, said Ben Pink Dandelion, Quakerism had become much more a religion of the perhaps, a perhaps which at times was almost absolute. For many, there was still an implicit belief that people could be guided by God, the 'perhapsness' was about things such as the Trinity and the nature of God.

There was also a strong feeling against being dogmatic in any way. 'If you were to say "Eureka, I've got the answer for everybody!",' he said, 'Quakers would say "you might be happier somewhere else".' He made it sound like a religion of scrupulous doubt.

When, by contrast, it comes to the *causes* that Quakers espouse, there is scarcely a murmur of dissent. Green issues of all kinds, total opposition to war and the preparation for it, help for HIV–Aids sufferers in Africa, aid for asylum seekers, support for gay marriage, there are no perhapses here.

Theirs has, in many ways, become a canon of good causes rather than beliefs. If, on the other hand, a critic were tempted to sneer that this is the ultimate in right-on religion, Quakers would retort that, for them, all these issues have a profound spiritual significance.

If a Friend was sent to jail for stealing a meeting's funds, the reaction more than likely would be to try to help the thief rather than kick him out, said Ben Pink Dandelion. If, on the other hand, a Friend wrote letters to newspapers that were critical of gays or Muslims, they might very well be asked to leave. That, it seems, would be the modern Quaker equivalent of a sin against the Holy Ghost.

'We are', he went on, 'entirely united in how to live in this world, trying to further God's purposes through justice and peace. And we are very this-worldly. We want to build the Kingdom now. We don't have much of a theology of the after-life.'

Quakers, though pacifist, are more than capable of promoting their causes in a thoroughly muscular way, as I had found with the lady selling *Peace News*. They are quite ready to go to jail for their beliefs, and did so most recently for withholding taxes which would have helped fund the Armed Services.

Deborah Filgate was arrested several times in America for taking part in demonstrations in favour of civil rights and against the Vietnam War. When asked by a policeman what her religion was, she replied that she was a Quaker – and watched him write down 'Communist sympathiser'.

In Britain, silence is still central to Quaker worship in 500 local meetings. Globally, it is a very different story, and Ben Pink Dandelion estimates that only 15 per cent of Quakers around the world now meet entirely in silence.

In Kenya, which has roughly a third of the world's Quakers, there might be no silence whatever in a meeting. They have been influenced by evangelical Quakers who had moved away from the practise. 'They saw silence in terms of waiting for God', said Ben Pink Dandelion, 'and, because they felt they had God already, couldn't see the point of it.'

In the United States, too, where there are 100,000 Quakers, you can go to meetings where there is as little as 20 minutes' silence in a 90-minute service, and sometimes none at all. A good many are led by pastors and include either a sermon or message.

In these and other places, even the Quaker reverence for silence and its value has not been proof against the modern world's addiction to talk and noise.

In Britain and some parts of the United States, by contrast, silence still holds absolute sway and still yields profound and unique blessings to believers and non-believers alike who regard it as both the quintessence of Quaker practise and the womb of deep spiritual experience.

For people like Deborah Filgate, a meeting that was not held in silence simply would not be a meeting for worship. 'I have found over a number of years', she said, 'that I know the people who come to our Wednesday meeting in a way that I would never have done if we had talked to each other. Yes, silence communicates.

'And you should know that, after one of our meetings, the oldest member – a man of 95 – spoke and simply thanked us for the quality of the silence.'

For Ben Pink Dandelion, silence is nothing less than the key 'to having a right relationship with God and a direct encounter with Him. It gives us the ability to listen to what God wants of us. I'd find it much more difficult if meetings were full of other, outward things.'

'When I go to a meeting,' said Margaret Osborne, 'I'm seeking the Light that I believe comes from God, and I can't find that light without my silence. I just can't see it if there's noise.'

12

Better than bullets

Anyone who still believes that silence is a complete waste of time might be given pause by what a small and unusual group of people who live in and around Beirut have been trying to do for their troubled country on the basis of what comes to them in silence.

In one way, the problems of the Lebanon are enough to reduce anyone to silence. For decades now it has been mercilessly preyed upon by its more powerful neighbours. The Syrians, the Israelis and the Iranians have all had their grubby fingers deep in the Lebanese pie.

From 1975 to 1990, moreover, the country was torn apart by a bitter and brutal civil war. Many of the buildings in the middle of Beirut are still pitted with shell- and bullet-holes. Nor is its present situation any less fraught. It could, at any moment, tip over again into conflict and chaos.

The Sunnis and Shias in its Muslim community are bitterly divided, and so are their Christian counterparts. It is a miracle that the Lebanon has survived in one piece thus far. If any nation stands in need of a thoroughgoing reconciliation between its different communities (and there are officially 18 of them), the Lebanon is surely that nation.

The men and women I went to Beirut to meet are admirably qualified for such a daunting task in one way at least: they are an incredibly diverse bunch. They include two men, one a Sunni Muslim, the other an Orthodox Christian, who were leaders on opposite sides in the civil war. Both are quite open about the fact that they have had a great deal of blood on their hands.

Among the others in the group are two Shia Muslims, a Maronite – Eastern Catholic – brother and sister, a Maronite lawyer and his secretary, a judge from the Druze community, a Mennonite, an American Jesuit priest, a distinguished academic and a man from the Greek Orthodox church. Palestinians from the refugee camps have also joined the group on occasions. The moving spirit behind it all is a cautious and deeply thoughtful Maronite lawyer called Ramez Salamé.

It was Salamé who started the group almost 30 years ago. He had become intrigued with the ideas of a body called Initiatives of Change and, in particular, with their practise of having regular times of silence. They claimed that, during these periods of silence, God could 'speak' to people.

At that point, Salamé had no religious faith of any kind but, as he persevered with the practise, 'silence became the space through which God came alive in my life'. He did not keep up his contact with Initiatives of Change (IofC) – he felt they were asking too much of him – but did continue with regular times of silence.

When the civil war began in 1975, he joined the Christian side and acquired a rifle, but found, before too long, that he was not cut out for the military life. Then he came across Christ's saying that 'my kingdom is not of this world' and realised that, although he was risking his life, he was not doing so for the kingdom of which Christ spoke. He began to feel a deep wish to join the fight for *that* Kingdom. At first, he had no idea how to begin, apart from the persistent thought that he should give up his rifle. A few days after he had handed it in, he felt that he ought to try to meet his old Muslim friends, lawyers with whom he had worked before the war but who were now behind enemy lines in West Beirut.

It was, he knew, an extremely risky venture – he had heard of people who had gone to the other side and never been seen again – but, when he telephoned his old friends, he discovered that they were only too willing to meet. He found the first journey, by taxi, absolutely terrifying, but none the less went back to see them several times, and that is how the process of dialogue began.

He was, at first, hesitant to make contact with the Initiatives of Change people again, but a Canadian Catholic priest whom he was seeing regularly told him that, in his view, he was called to work with them. He made up his mind to take the advice, invited some of his old Initiatives of Change (IofC) friends to Beirut and, together, they decided to start a series of regular meetings which would be open to people from all the different communities.

To Salamé's surprise, those meetings have now been going on for almost three decades. 'Many times', he said, 'I thought to myself this will probably be the last meeting. Often nothing outstanding or dramatic took place during the meetings and I wondered whether people wouldn't begin to get bored, but they have never stopped.'

The meetings take place in a building close to his office. Between ten and 20 people come every two weeks. The form of the meetings is simple enough, but the content is thoroughly unusual.

After brief opening remarks, the group spends 15 to 20 minutes in complete silence, trying, as they put it, 'to listen to God' and, in some part, reflecting on their own lives when measured against absolute standards of honesty, purity, unselfishness and love. They then share any thoughts they have had with complete candour.

'People', said Salamé, 'will share where they themselves need to change, in their families and professions, for example, things which need to be different, things to be put right. We share these things in an atmosphere of complete trust and, since there are both men and women present, the sharing has to be discreet.'

'The quality of real honesty is not a common thing but, fortunately, we have it in our meetings. The personal friendships we have built up over the years are based on a common willingness to be open about our lives, to be honest about our needs and failures.'

'That is the quality of our friendship and it has that depth because of the silence and the absolute moral standards which are the basis of everything, though not explicitly so. For me, silence does not have any supernatural quality, but it is a necessary space for us to connect with the Truth.'

'I also have a belief that society cannot change for the better unless human nature changes dramatically, unless we overcome our selfishness and pride. Our focus in the group is that that change needs to take place in ourselves first. Without that, we can't hope for anything better in our country.' It is a perfect statement of Gandhi's dictum that we should try to be the change we want to see in the world.

'I like Christ's words in the Gospel to the young man who was on his way to the Temple', Salamé went on. 'Stop, he tells him, there is another priority; go first and reconcile yourself with your brother!'

'For me, that means I have to try to repair the wrong I may have done – which requires a lot of courage. That willingness to confess where I have been wrong and to try to put it right is the key to peace in the world. That spirit has created our basic fellowship and it has made other initiatives possible.'

'The Christians in our group don't have the same understanding of times of silence as our Muslim friends. For them, God doesn't speak, He inspires. They prefer the idea of waiting for God's inspiration.'

'When people in the group share what has come to them in a time of silence, there is no comment from the others. If there were to be comment, other people might not have the chance to say what they have to say. We only meet for an hour and a half and we want everyone to have that chance. What is more, the silence of good friends is comment enough and gives God the chance to speak to them directly.'

'We also don't spend time talking about politics, because that could create a division among us. We have thought about it and, for honesty's sake, will sometimes say where we are coming from politically, but we wouldn't dwell on it.

'These meetings of ours have proved to be a preparation for other things. Because of our personal experience of change and reconciliation over the years, we have felt that we could do something for the bigger situation. We have tried to spread the spirit we have found and many others have joined us.'

'We usually end our meeting with improvised prayers. A Muslim may begin, then a Christian will continue.'

In 1984, with the civil war still raging, it was obvious that there was a desperate need for dialogue between the Lebanon's different communities, and Salamé and his friends decided to do something about it. They launched a series of annual meetings where that dialogue could take place. In the early years, when the country was still deeply fragmented and it was impossible to move around safely, they had to go to Cyprus to hold the meetings.

The need was obvious, the response enthusiastic. Ministers, Muslim religious leaders, bishops, judges and MPs came. Some flew via Damascus, others came by ship from the port of Jounieh. They then spent several days together, and talked candidly about the situation in the country. Some came again and again, others went off and formed groups of their own. Bridges were built. The meetings had a fundamental effect on many people's lives.

Sailing back to Jounieh after one dialogue, Salamé heard Pope John Paul 2 on the radio appealing to Lebanese Christians 'to be a leaven of reconciliation and unity', and thought to himself, 'Well, that is what we are trying to do.'

By this time, the group had begun to attract some very surprising people. One of them was Assaad Shaftari, who had been the deputy director of intelligence on the Christian side in the civil war. After a bitter split in the Christian ranks, he had moved with his family to the town of Zahlé in the Bekaa Valley and, for some time, his life was in danger from those who had once been his comrades-in-arms.

They tried five times to kill him – once with a rocket-propelled grenade, once with a bomb – and took over his home and office.

It was in Zahlé that he and his wife first came across this group who spoke about wanting both peace and change. They met in people's homes or in the residence of the Maronite Bishop. Shaftari was highly suspicious, assuming that – like everyone else in the Lebanon – they had another, hidden agenda.

'What they were preaching sounded very positive,' he said, 'and I thought "I'm here in the bishop's residence and these people want to change the world, but I want Lebanon to be the way *I* want it, entirely Christian, with all the Muslims thrown out. I want them to go back to their camels." A lot of Lebanese Christians thought like me.'

'The next question that came up at their meetings, of course, was "are you ready to change?" and I replied that I had nothing I needed to change. I was great and I felt great. As for the four standards they talked about, I said "I'm completely honest and pure, I'm ashamed of nothing. When it came to love, I said I had no problem with that, I loved those who loved me – and I didn't have to love the ones I hated.'

'Look, I was a young boss with guns and bodyguards and people telling me I was great all the time, so it was easy to imagine that I was perfect. And those people in the group never gave a direct answer to a question. They just listened to me, gave me some good example and then left me to decide how I was going to live. They never pushed me – never.'

'Then of course came the business of silence. OK, I was used to praying and meditating. I used to go on the first Thursday of every month to sit for two hours in church and adore the Blessed Sacrament. But then I heard from these people that prayer was not meant to be a one-way conversation.'

'I'd always said things to God – "I need, I want, I miss, I would like" – and then there was a bit of adoring, "please bless my life" and so on. Most of it was demands really. Now, for the first time, I heard of the idea of listening to God. That was entirely new for me.'

'When I first tried to have one of their times of silence, I just couldn't do it. It was hell. I was overwhelmed by so many thoughts that I had to run away. I had to face my enormous ego, the fact that I had so many wrong things in me. I didn't find that easy to accept.'

'Facing the sins that I committed during the war came much later. For me, at that time, they were acceptable sins which I had done in the name of my country, my Christianity and my community. I had put up a wall inside to seal those things off, to keep them in the corner where they belonged.'

'Anyway, after that first time of silence, I tried to avoid being by myself. I made sure that I was always surrounded by people, and I always had the TV or radio turned on at their loudest, because I suspected where sitting in silence would take me. And when I did have times of silence, I just let my conscience deal with very small issues in my character. I kept God limited to one area of my life. I said to Him "that's enough for you!"'

'Even in times of silence, you know, you can – so to speak – avoid having a really open mind. There are lots of tricks I can teach you if you like! When it comes round to sharing your thoughts, instead of being honest about yourself, you can – as I did – share general theories about honesty and unselfishness. In those early days, I behaved as if I didn't know that there was a very large dark side within me.'

That dark side included the fact that, during the war, Shaftari had been directly responsible for the death of a great many people, more than he cared to think about. 'When you kill someone', he said, 'you always kill part of yourself too.' And when you became a killing machine and stopped feeling anything, that was the most dangerous part of all.

For a long time, though attending the meetings of the group in both Zahlé and, later, Beirut, he avoided facing that dark side, but, as time went on, the area in which he allowed God to work grew larger and larger. 'That process', he added, 'is still going on today, it never stops, I'm a human being.' Eventually, he felt driven to go to confession.

'You can't easily do that in the Orthodox church', he said, 'and although I talked about my problems in the group, I couldn't confess there because they couldn't give me absolution, so I found a Maronite priest who was ready to hear my confession. I went to him many times.'

Shaftari is sure that he would never have got to that point had he not been part of a group whose members were so honest about their own failings.

By this time, Salamé was beginning to organise the group's dialogue meetings and Shaftari knew that there would be Muslims there. 'I realised', he said, 'that we would have to be open and say what was in our hearts, so I drew up a long list of all the things I had against the Muslims. They were on the side of the Palestinians, they were pro-Arab, they didn't believe in the Lebanon as the final shape of our country – and they were killing us!

'I went there ready to shoot out my list. To my surprise, I discovered that the Muslims had an even longer list about the Christians. Being with the Muslims, of course, I got to know them better. I used to refer to Muslims as "them" or "those". Now I discovered they had names – Mohammed, Ali, Hassan and so on.'

'Slowly, slowly over the years, I learned to accept what they said, to understand it and even love most of it. When, later, some incident happened in the country, I tried to look at it through their eyes. I even had times of silence with some of them and we shared our thoughts – just imagine that!'

'These days I have a very inclusive idea about the Lebanon. I accept that, like it or not, it's an Arab country – we speak Arabic after all – and that we are not Phoenician or French. My father can still sing the Marseillaise all the way through. And I see that Phoenician is not an identity which applies exclusively to Christians. The Muslims are Phoenicians too.

Then, one day, Shaftari heard that one of his son's friends had told him that, whenever he went near a mosque, he felt utterly disgusted. Shaftari remembered himself at the same age and realised afresh that these were feelings that were being passed down from generation to generation. What, he wondered, could he do about it?

In one of his times of silence, the idea occurred to him of writing an open letter to the Lebanese people explaining what he had done in the war, offering an apology for it and declaring that he was ready to put right whatever he could.

'I wasn't at all sure about the idea', he said. 'It could have been very dangerous for me, my family and my friends. So I asked Ramez what he thought about it. He never answered. He smiled and nodded, but that was it.'

'I went home, sat in my office and wrote three pages in three minutes though I'm not very good at classical Arabic. I gave it to my wife and asked what she thought. "Who wrote it?," she asked. "I did, and I'd like to have it published," ' I replied. "I'm 100 per cent with you, she said."

'I took it to the press agency but, for some reason, it didn't get published. On the fifth day, I rang to find out why. That night I had a phone call from some comrades in the war. "You need to withdraw that letter," they told me. So I reminded them that I hadn't said "we," that it was purely personal. They said they'd come back to me, so then I cut off all the phones and went ahead.' The letter was published among others in *Al Nahar*, a leading newspaper. It was headed 'An open letter to my victims'.

There was little response from the Christian side, but the impact among Muslims and Palestinians in particular was considerable. The head of the Sûreté Générale, a Muslim intelligence service, telephoned Assaad to express his appreciation. The letter has not made Shaftari popular, but it has earned him a measure of respect.

Since then, he has spent a good part of his life trying to keep his promise to make amends for what he did in the war. He goes to schools and universities to talk about his experience and the way he has tried to change. He is one of the coordinators of a group of 26 NGOs that work for peace. 'No one', he said, 'speaks about the war, we almost have a state of amnesia about it, but I've taken part in campaigns to tell young people what civil war is really like.' Many of them have thanked him because their parents had not told them anything.

He may have been given absolution, but he still grieves every day about what he did. 'I'm still suffering', he said. 'People have said "You confessed, why should you suffer?" I suffer because I can't bring them back."

'I grieve particularly for those who suffered torture, I don't have the answer to these dilemmas. The people I speak of are dead, their parents are getting older and that only doubles my sense of guilt. I suffer when I hear of a child carrying a gun and I say to myself "we just haven't done enough!" '

Shaftari finds being part of a group whose members are candid about their own failures and shortcomings invaluable. 'You know that, if you fail, you can always go to one of your friends to ask for help. It's a kind of honest community – and that makes us free to do bigger things.'

One of his closest friends in the group is a Sunni Muslim who became part of it some years after he did. It is a friendship in which a shared experience of war and the value of silence play a considerable part. It is also a friendship which neither would ever have conceived possible.

Mohieddin Shihab became *mukhtar* (Mayor is the nearest approximation) of an important district in Beirut in 1995 and has just been re-elected for the fourth time. He is proud of the fact that he is the descendant of a sacred family – the mother of the Prophet came from his tribe – and of the fact that his roots are 'full of Arab dignity and Islamic teaching'.

He was only 18 when the civil war erupted. Coming from a noble family, whose forbears had helped Saladin defeat the Crusaders, he immediately joined one of the Muslim militias and, despite his youth, soon became a leader.

'I used to plan the tactics,' he said, 'and it was me who took the decisions when we had made up our minds what to attack. More than 100 Shihabs fought in our area alone. It was a very bloody, ruthless war. We often fought in the streets with knives and gun butts. Many of my comrades died and, with everyone who went, the passion for revenge became all the greater.'

'I myself committed many atrocities of all kinds. In 1976, we were ordered to attack a small town called Aldamour some 30 kilometres south of Beirut in retaliation for Christian attacks. We wiped that town off the map of Lebanon and I wrote on the sign which bore the town's name the word Almodamara – which means "the destroyed city."'

'The things I did live with you for your whole life. I fought for 13 years. I didn't only fight against the Christians, I fought against the Israelis during their first invasion in 1978 and then again in 1982, when they occupied Beirut for seven days. I was the one who launched the resistance for the whole of the city. We hunted them as you would hunt bears. I was wounded three times.'

'In those years, I lost my life and I felt as if I had lost my future. I only started thinking about my future when I was 33 years old – to find work, to get married.'

'It was then – after all the blood and corpses I had seen, all the atrocities I had committed – that I began to wonder whether what we had done was right or wrong. I asked myself questions about life, religion, destiny and about all those who had died – why had all of that happened?'

'I asked myself whether all the Christians were as anti-Muslim as we had painted them, and so my younger cousin Hisham and I began to go into the Christian areas to find out for ourselves. I had always imagined that the Christians were rich, spoke French, were well-educated and pro-Israeli. I actually *wanted* to find Christians who hated Muslims so that I could tell myself that all we had done in the war was fully justified. Then I could sleep comfortably.'

'But I found that the Christians were often just as poor, if not poorer, than Muslims, that they didn't speak French and weren't so well-educated, that 90 per cent of them were not pro-Israeli. All that completely shocked me. I knew then that I had been on a wrong way.'

'I couldn't bring back to life all those who were killed in battle with me, but I decided that I had to try to make sure that such things never happened again in my country.'

Shihab, like Shaftari, started to work for reconciliation. In 1993 he set up an organisation that aimed 'to stretch out our hands to Christians throughout Beirut and to help the poor among them.' It proved to be remarkably successful in the years before the turn of the century. By that time, he had been elected Mayor for the first time.

'Then', said Shihab, 'my cousin Hisham had a call from someone called Ramez. I refused to respond because I thought it was some Christian preaching group, and I told Hisham to tell them to go and preach elsewhere.'

'But Hisham didn't agree, he said we had nothing to lose by meeting them. If we found a clergyman there, we could just say goodbye. He came back from a meeting and told me that they weren't preaching, that they respected Islam very much, that this was something quite different from anything he had ever seen before, though he didn't fully understand it.'

'Anyway, he attended their meetings for a year and told me that among them was this man Assaad Shaftari – who I'd heard about in the war – and that he was completely changed. But he insisted that it was not this group's aim to convert people, just to help you practise your own religion as you should practise it.'

'He spoke about their four criteria, and I didn't find them at all strange because I thought they were common to all religions, but then there was this business about a time of silence. Hisham spoke about it with enthusiasm, but I wondered what it was, because we don't have a silence time in Islam.'

'That question was still unsolved when I went to Ramez's place for the first time in 2000. I felt I had to solve the problem or not go again, but the silent time isn't something you can teach, you have to feel it.'

'I believe, from my own experience, that those who have suffered most in their lives have a better chance of catching the idea. I tried three or four times before I was able to catch it and, when that happened, I felt God was opening a new aspect in my life which I had never discovered before.'

'Does it need someone who has big problems to get hold of the idea? I don't know, but I was carrying on my shoulders all the atrocities I had done. Anyway, in that third or fourth attempt at a silent time, I felt God guiding me to know what I should do. He began to give me ideas, just as a lighthouse gives instructions to a ship – "watch out, here there are rocks but there is the port." '

'As I went on trying to practise the silent time, I became more professional in recognising what was coming from God and what was just my own thinking. "Go to the meeting at 2.30," or something like that, that's just organising the routine of the day, it's not an instruction from God.'

'But if I think "today you spoke to your brother in a rude way and he is angry, so go and see him this evening and make it right," that is not normal and I know it is from God. A silent time gives a person many advantages. It lights a candle in your dark spirit, it gives you a space in which your spirit can renew itself.'

'In the first five minutes of a silent time I feel I am healing my spirit from the injuries and pressures of the day. Work, money, all those kinds of worries. In those early moments, my spirit is scattered all over the place, but then I am able to regather myself, to become myself again. Then I start to feel relaxed and hear the instruction of God.'

'These days, I practise the silent time for an hour every morning. I get up at five, do the morning prayer, read the Koran, have coffee and then go to the office. From seven until eight, the door is closed. At eight, I open it to the public.'

'I carry out the easier instructions I receive as soon as I can. For example, to ring Ramez to ask if we shouldn't do the dialogue conference differently, or to say sorry to someone. I like to do that immediately. But then there are things which are more spiritual than practical. To make sure to pray five times a day, not just four. Then, since we were going to have a dialogue with Christians about the place of Jesus and Mary in the Koran, I needed to speak to a sheikh so I could do it in an accurate way.'

'The silent time doesn't just work, it is the driving wheel of our lives. It gives you, in the morning, the whole instruction from God about how you should behave in your daily life. Sometimes the instructions are clear and I don't carry them out very well – but that's normal, because we are human!'

'For me, those instructions do not come from a voice, though it may be so for some people, it's more an overwhelming feeling. It starts in your mind and then goes to your heart. In many ways, that overwhelming feeling is stronger than a voice and you don't just hear it in your ears. At turning points in your life, you may hear a "voice," but the overwhelming feeling you can always have.'

Extraordinary, I thought to myself, for someone who had been so doubtful about the whole idea of silence. Shihab makes the practise sound so simple and natural. He has even written a pamphlet about it, with the title *Rissalat Al Samt* (The Message of Silence).

'In our group', he went on, 'we don't practise the silent time just for the sake of it, but to try to change ourselves as the beginning of a change in society and our country. Otherwise it's just personal – and then you can go back to sleep!' For him, the scale of the Lebanon's needs makes a merely personal religion seem not only narrow and inadequate but also rather contemptible.

'My office is like a beehive in trying to change the country. All the people know how I was and what I have become. If I obey God in my job, change takes place in the community. For me, there's no cheating, no under-the-counter compromises, no spending money to buy votes. I don't pay money to anyone. To be honest is better than buying people. It's made me a 100 per cent better Muslim.'

'Being with Ramez and Assaad in the group is enjoyable. We have harmony, and I trust them 100 per cent. We go together to schools and universities, we share in NGO activities, we try in everything we do to play our part in rebuilding the country. Assaad and myself have made a film for UNESCO about what has happened to us and what we do together. He and I are now dear friends. We spent 15 days in America, travelling and speaking together.'

To Shaftari, the growth in their friendship seems almost unreal. The place where his son works is only five minutes' walk from Shihab's office, and the mayor has told him that, if there were to be any breakdown in community relations, he would shelter Shaftari's son in his own home.

'When he said that,' said Shaftari, 'it felt like something from Kafka. He has gone from being my enemy to being ready to protect my son!'

Shihab, of course, is more aware than anyone just how fragile the situation in Lebanon still is. 'It's critical,' he said, 'and it will remain critical for another five years or so. To begin with, there is the possibility of an Israeli war against Hezbollah. Then there is a real danger of a civil war between Sunni and Shia Muslims.'

'So we have to continue to build up trust, to build bridges. We need to put in much more effort if we are to avoid another civil war. The divisions between Muslims are bigger and more dangerous than the divisions in the Christian communities.'

Everyone in the group feels that they could do much better. 'I don't think it's realistic to strive for a total solution to Lebanon's problems,' said Ramez Salamé. 'That is something which God may give, but you can't just pluck it out of the air. We have tried to be a leaven of goodness, and perhaps we have been able to create a little brook of reconciliation in our country, but we also need to see where we have failed.'

'We are just trying to make ourselves available to God', said Shaftari. 'As for results, I don't know and I don't care. Either you are trying to work for God or you become God yourself. I don't even want to ask the question. I'd rather leave what happens to Him.'

'I certainly feel we could do so much better, but I do meet a thousand students every year and, if I can manage to save one young man who might otherwise turn to war, that is enough for me.'

They are a small group, Ramez and his friends, but their faithfulness and persistence over more than three decades has already produced some notable results. Over the years, they have also won many sympathisers in high places – politicians, judges, officials of the central bank – people who do not attend their meetings but believe in what they are doing.

Who knows, this little network of honesty and trust, forged in silence, may yet be of use in one of Lebanon's dark hours.

13

The rigours of Zen

A friendly Zen nun called Rosemary had invited me to a *zazen* – a sitting – in the middle of Oxford and, knowing little or nothing about Zen, I thought it would be no bad thing to start at the sharp end. I was in for a surprise, indeed several surprises.

That evening, there were eight people at the sitting – three women, including Rosemary, and five men, dressed either very informally or in a sort of robe. We had all taken our shoes and socks off.

The room was very precisely laid out, with black mats called *zafutons* in a square on the floor of the meditation area, and black cushions called *zafus* behind each one. In the centre was an altar with candles, flowers and a black statuette of the Buddha.

Since I could not splay out my knees sufficiently to take up the lotus position on the floor, Rosemary pointed me towards a chair and gave me some hurried instructions about how I should sit when the *zazen* began. She showed me how I should set my feet and indicated that my hands should be placed one on top of the other with the tips of the thumbs touching, and then rest them on my thighs.

I should step into the meditation area with my left foot first and I should then bow with my hands together. That was to be followed by more bows. I should have my eyes half-open and look down. There is clearly nothing *ad hoc* or free-and-easy about Zen practise.

After bowing to my cushion and to the people on the other side of the room, as I had been told, I sat down on my *zafu* and, like the others, turned round to face the wall. The idea, Rosemary had said, was to go beyond thought, and I found it perfectly easy to sit still and let such thoughts as I had flit across my mind. It was very relaxing, but rather boring.

Occasionally, a bell would tinkle but, apart from that, there was complete silence except when Rosemary murmured that we should be aware of our breath because that would help us 'come into the present moment'. After about half an hour we all got up, and a brief spell of walking meditation – called *kin hin* – began, during which we all moved slowly round the room in a sort of circle. I felt thoroughly clumsy, not being accustomed to move at that rather stately pace.

There was then another half-hour of *zazen*, again in almost complete silence, apart from a suggestion by Rosemary that we might open our eyes if we felt sleepy. She told me afterwards that she had said that because she was falling asleep herself. The *zazen* ended with chanting in a language entirely alien to me, which turned out to be a mixture of ancient Chinese and Japanese.

Then, after an absolute minimum of social chit-chat, people just drifted away. At no point had there been much feeling of real warmth or fellowship, and certainly no obvious sense of joyfulness. We had all been marooned in our own private space. It was clearly all about the practise and as unlike a collective religious occasion of the sort I was used to as I could possibly imagine.

That, moreover, as I discovered when I talked to Rosemary later, is exactly how it was intended to be. 'We don't want people to come for social reasons', she said. 'It's to do with the fact that the practise involves rooting yourself in inner silence, and a lot of chat before and afterwards just wouldn't help.'

Individual relationships, whether people got on with each other or not, could be quite a distraction. Wearing simple robes, too, both helped people look the same and made them less inclined to think about their individual personalities and personal relationships.

She herself did not necessarily know those who came. She certainly did not ask what they did, she was there just to help them practise.

Another reason why people were not encouraged to talk was that it was bound to raise expectations. Surely, though, that was a good thing? 'No', replied Rosemary, 'because if they talked about what they were finding in the practise, the other people might ask themselves "why is he having that great experience and I'm not?!" '

So what was it all about? Were the people who came seeking some sort of enlightenment? Rosemary replied that, in her form of Zen – Soto, a school founded in the ninth century – the practise itself was thought of as enlightenment. They were not seeking it. They already had it.

In starting to practise, she went on, you should not be looking for anything for yourself, nor should you have any specific expectations. The practise was part of a transforming discipline in which you were seeking to transcend the ego in inner silence.

'In Zen', she went on, 'there are two selves. There is the true self, which is what we find in inner silence and which connects us with other people, and then there is the other self with all our personal ideas, which are about getting happiness and other things for ourselves.'

Then, quite suddenly, she stopped. She had already answered more questions than she ought to have done, she said. Why, I asked? 'Because the more you try to explain,' she replied, 'the more you are closing the other person's mind. That's because language is part of the ego.'

Anyway, she went on, relenting, inner silence was the heart of the whole thing. It allowed us to be less caught up in ideas and thoughts that masked reality and created delusion. Inner silence helped us to stop being controlled by the ego all the time.

There are many varieties of Buddhism but, in all of them, silence is the arena, the battleground, where bliss, enlightenment and liberation from the ego are hoped for and sought, often with a dedication and intensity so astonishing as to make a run-of-the-mill Christian feel like a limp and pallid creature.

Zen seems to have a particular attraction for the more cerebral Western mind, perhaps partly because it delights in enigmas, paradoxes and riddles. Its practitioners are apt to parry inquiries by throwing a question back in the questioner's face. 'What is the heart of Zen?' I asked one man. 'What is the heart of Graham?' he replied, irritatingly.

For those who have no other faith, Zen carries none of the – to them – unattractive entanglements of a belief in God with all the received dogmas that are apt to go with it. For those who do have another faith, the practise of Zen often seems to involve no contradictions. 'It's like pouring gin into tonic or tonic into gin', explained an Anglo-Catholic who is also a regular Zen practitioner.

'I am a professing Christian', he went on, 'and, in the past, I had read many religious books which spoke about real prayer being silence. The trouble was that my own prayer life didn't reflect what I was reading about.' Now he seeks to sit in 'pure silence' because, he says, 'silence is where truth lies.' So, I said, you find truth in silence? 'Or does truth find me?' he replied.

What, though, I wondered, had the people at the *zazen* got out of it? I stopped a man going off into the night and asked what he had made of it – expecting, I must admit, a rather negative response. I could not have been more wrong.

Zen, he replied, with eyes that shone in the lamplight, had transformed his life; it had made him tremendously happy. Having always had the gravest doubt about anything spiritual, Zen had shown him that the 'awakening' which it promised was purely physiological. And silence was the key to Zen, the heart of the whole thing.

The enthusiasm poured out of him in an unstoppable flood and, before I knew it, we were drinking coffee together in a handy city-centre bar. Mike spoke of human beings being able, through the practise of Zen, to switch from the egocentric to the allocentric pathways of the brain, of being freed from the constraints of time and self, of by-passing those areas of the brain which promoted egocentric action.

He illustrated the point by talking about the way we drive on motorways, with the ego constantly urging us to put our foot down. In that state of mind, he said, you were aware only of the cars in front of you and your overwhelming desire to get past them – but seeing nothing at all of the wider world.

Zen, by contrast, led you off into a quiet side road, where you could begin to appreciate all the glories of the world around you, where you were no longer driven by the ego.

With some forms of Zen, he went on, it could take years to achieve the 'awakening' he was speaking of. The Soto variety came into that category, though he enjoyed its *zazens*. With the *rinzai* variety, whose origins dated back to the seventh century and which he preferred, it was possible to achieve it within as little as seven weeks. To do that, its Japanese practitioners did sometimes use methods which were admittedly brutal – for example, hitting people across the shoulders with a stick called a *kyosaku* if they showed signs of losing focus or falling asleep during *zazen* – but it did the job. He was quite prepared to accept discipline of that kind and could not wait to go to Japan.

'The awakening', when it came, lasted only a very short time – between seven and fifteen seconds, he said – but it made everything seem worthwhile because it gave you a sense of being united with the entire planet. You were never the same again.

He spoke like the most gung-ho of born-again Christians. I had never met a more enthusiastic convert. Yet Mike is no spaced-out oddball, but the son of a Staffordshire bricklayer. He had become a commercial airline pilot after flying Vampire jets in the Royal Air Force. He is also delightful company.

Another, much larger Zen group that meets in a semi-detached house in North Oxford has added a strong dash of *rinzai* onto a base of Soto practise. In particular, they make use of *koans* – riddles that admit of no logical analysis – to help their devotees reach awakening and 'realise their true selves'.

At the *zazen* I blundered into there, the *roshi* (or teacher) was giving what, in other circumstances, might have been called a sermon. A Zen master of the tenth or eleventh century, he said, had been answering questions from one of his monks. The monk had asked him what was the body of wisdom. The master had answered: 'The oyster swallows the moonlight.'

At that time in China, the *roshi* explained, people believed that oysters came to the surface at night, opened their 'jaws' and the moonlight went in – creating pearls. The monk had then asked, 'What is the activity of wisdom?' and the Zen master had answered: 'A rabbit becomes pregnant.' Which, said the master, was a way of expressing the constant creativity of the universe. It was rather like listening to a poetically-inclined vicar trying to make sense of one of the more obscure passages of the Old Testament.

The *roshi* then went on to say that, during the group's recent five-day *sesshin* – or retreat – they had been seeking to pass through five different levels of silence. The first, easy for two days but much harder for five, was not to speak to each other. The second level was not to talk to themselves.

The third was to achieve a total absence of self, so that there was no one there to talk to. The fourth was even beyond that, what he called 'a state of pure energy'. And the last was a kind of silence that gave them a sense of the oneness of the universe. That, he said, was the real fruit of a deep inner silence.

The *sesshin*, which had been held at a Catholic priory on the outskirts of the city, was clearly no light-hearted affair. The first sitting began at 6.15 in the morning, the last started after dinner, at 8.45 in the evening. 'That', said a man who had been there, with some feeling, 'is an awful lot of *zazen*.' For those who asked for it, the *kyosaku* was in ever-present use to keep them up to the mark.

Despite all their efforts, however, not all the retreaters seem to have achieved the awakening they had been seeking. 'I know what I'm aiming for,' said one, 'but I keep being told that I'm just missing by a very little bit.' Was it rather like the Lottery then, I asked? 'Yes,' he replied with a laugh. 'It is very hard to get that last number.' The Carmelite priests who were their hosts were profoundly impressed both by the ardour of their practise and by their impeccable behaviour.

Even the day-long meetings at the North Oxford house, which involve a mere five hours of *zazen*, have an intensity and stringency which you can feel as soon as you enter the meditation area. I have never felt its like in any Christian church or Islamic mosque. There was, as before, much prayerful joining of hands, much bowing and prostration, much solemnity. It was a highly ritualised ceremony and there was a pleasant smell of incense in the air. Never, I thought, a goal more ardently pursued: the very opposite of the rather limp discussions I have taken part in during Lent in Anglican churches.

Truth to tell, I felt as if I was trespassing on a very intense and private occasion. I failed the *kin hin* test yet again, out of rhythm, out of step, out of everything. The participants were clearly not best pleased to have a clumsy intruder fouling up their devotions. Since they had come from as far afield as Stafford and Ipswich to be there, I could quite understand.

Before too long, I retired in some haste. If the silence of those present had spoken, it would surely have breathed a grateful collective 'Good riddance!'

Having caught a flavour of the rigour of Zen practise, I began to wonder what a *sesshin*, and particularly one of the *rinzai* variety, was like. I was fortunate. My friend Mike, having been unable, for one reason or another, to go to Japan, had as second best signed up for a *sesshin*, to be held at a large Victorian house near Wimborne in Dorset.

It had, he told me when he came back, been an astonishing and, in the end, exhilarating experience, and was more than happy to tell me all about it. I found his account astonishing. I had never heard anything stranger, or more intriguing.

The *sesshin*, said Mike, had lasted for five days and been what he called 'a heavy-duty affair'. There were 28 of them there, and the man leading it was a highly-regarded Japanese Zen master called Shinzan Myomo Roshi, the abbot of the Guryoku Ji monastery. He had spoken for half an hour or so on their first evening, in very broken English. He was diminutive, his head was completely shaved and he had 'incredibly piercing, searching' eyes. Mike was plainly awed by his presence.

They were all told that the *sesshin* was to be held in total silence, that there should be no eye contact or talking between them, except for their one-to-one meetings with the *roshi*, which would take place early each morning. During the five days, they should wash and shower but not shave. Their mobiles had, of course, already been left behind.

They were also told that they were expected to be up by four in the morning, that the first meditation would begin at five and that they would go to bed at nine in the evening. There would be ten hours of formal meditation during the day in half-hour periods with ten-minute breaks in between; and 90 minutes of 'mindfulness work' which, given Mike's inherited bricklaying skills, involved helping to build a greenhouse; and an hour of Zen yoga.

Since they would not be talking to each other, or even making eye contact, that allowed them to meditate for 17 hours each day.

They were all given the same well-known *koan* to puzzle over and try to answer. One of the most famous Chinese Zen masters, Joshu Jushin, who was born in the eighth century, was once asked by one of his monks whether a dog had Buddha-nature, that is to say basic goodness within. Joshu replied with the single word 'mu', which means nothing or nothingness. The retreaters were asked to work out exactly what '*mu*' meant.

'There is', said Mike, 'no logical answer to a *koan*. It is designed to prevent you from seeking an intellectual solution to the question. Trying to resolve it is meant to force your brain out of its analytical left-hemisphere bias and into intuitive, right-hemisphere thinking.'

On the first morning, soon after five o'clock, Mike stood with a score or so of the other retreaters in a queue outside the Zen master's door. The procedure had already been spelt out to them in some detail. 'I was to ring the gong which stood outside his door twice', said Mike, 'and then, when a little bell sounded, I was to walk in, bow three times and fall on my knees before the *roshi*. You were told to look not at him but at the floor.'

Mike had been expecting a long interview and some detailed help in finding the answer to the *koan*. Instead, all that happened was that the master asked him 'show me *mu*'. Mike was lost for words. He said nothing. Within no more than 15 seconds, the Zen master had rung his bell again and Mike was asked to leave, bowing as he went.

He felt, not surprisingly, disappointed, let down, and angry with himself for not having tried hard enough to answer the question. He also felt convinced that he would never find the answer but, none the less, he was absolutely determined that he was not going to admit defeat. Seventeen hours of meditation lay ahead before his next encounter with the *roshi*.

Day Two, when he sometimes wondered whether he was going mad, was a repeat performance of that first, dismaying morning. Again the *roshi* asked him 'show me *mu*', but, hard as Mike tried to think what it might mean, he had no real insight into what he was trying to do or what he was supposed to be thinking. The *roshi*, he said, 'looked through me, saw my helpless posture, knew full well there was no hope of an answer and dismissed me.' This time, the interview had lasted 40 seconds.

Day Three was not all that different but, by that time, things had begun to happen inside Mike. 'I had fallen in love with silence', he said, 'and had begun to see what the purpose of Zen training is. It's to dissolve your ego.'

'It's as if we are in this stone house totally covered with ivy. It even covers the doors and windows so we can't see out at all. That's what our ego is like, and it can be destroyed if you chop it off at the roots. That is what Zen training aims to do.'

He had also, he went on, 'started to have a deep awareness of the word *mu*, so I responded much more quickly when, on the third morning, the *roshi* asked me yet again "what is *mu*?." With all the meditation, I had been going much more deeply into my sub-conscious and my awareness had grown.'

This time, the interview lasted for a full two minutes and the *roshi* advised Mike to go deeper. 'You are on the right path', he told him.

Mike sensed that the Zen master knew he was getting closer to an answer 'because of the way I was behaving. My replies were instantaneous, coming from deep inside. It wasn't cerebral any longer, it had become intuitive.' When he left the *roshi*, he felt elated for the first time.

He scarcely slept at all during the third night, but continued to meditate. He had come to the conclusion that *mu* was the energy of the universe, what scientists call the quantum field, but, when he went to see the *roshi* on the fourth morning, he failed miserably to express what he had concluded because he tried to do so in rational, scientific terms.

This time, though, the interview lasted for three minutes – and then the *roshi* told him to get hold of the interpreter, an English Zen master who was one of his aides. The Englishman told Mike that the *roshi* realised that he had grasped the answer to the *koan*, but had completely failed to convey that answer. 'How can I do it?' Mike asked. 'That', replied the English Zen master, 'is your problem, not mine, but don't hold back. And stay awake all night if you need to!'

Mike took his advice and scarcely slept at all during that fourth night. He spent most of the time meditating about what he would do when he saw the *roshi* for his final interview. He asked himself how he was going to explain what was in his mind to an 80-year-old Japanese with very poor English. He decided that the only way was to use actions instead of words. 'My plan', he said, 'was to shock him, to show him that I knew what *mu* was even if I didn't have the words.'

'When I went in at five', he recalled, 'I was absolutely fizzing with energy. I had realised that the *roshi* could sense how I was by the way I struck the gong so, this time, I didn't tap it lightly and rather nervously, I hit it very loudly and went in full of confidence. I had lost all my diffidence.

'When he said "show me *mu*," I picked up the first thing which came to hand, a chair, and slapped it down on the table by his side. It was the only way that I could demonstrate the energy which *mu* meant to me.'

'Then I banged the floor with my hand, so that there were vibrations through the earth. "This is *mu*', I said, "everything is *mu*'. The *roshi* was smiling for the first time. Then I rolled up the carpet which was in front of him and again hit the floor, this time with both my hands.'

'I gave the *roshi* my hands and said "here, feel them." The *roshi* put his hands in mine and smiled again. Then I pulled out a bunch of leaves that I'd put in my pocket, threw them on the floor and said "this is *mu*, everything is *mu*, the universe is *mu*."'

The *roshi* then asked Mike to sit down and asked him a series of questions, which he answered immediately and instinctively. The *roshi* told him, 'You have *mu*! I can pass you on the *mu koan*.' The interview had lasted a full six minutes.

Mike was so pumped up, so delighted, that he had to walk round the house for two hours because his energy level was so high. He felt he was about to explode. He was empty of thought but was thrilled to have found the answer to the riddle.

'That, you know, was my first *sesshin*', he said. 'In those first two days, there was so much silence that I felt suicidal. I couldn't come to terms with it, my ego longed to put things into words, but by the end of the *sesshin* I didn't want to start talking again.'

'There were so many wonderful experiences as the times of silence went on day after day. For one thing, the recognition of the power of my ego, how it leads you constantly astray. It was so marvellous to discover that fundamental truth, even though painfully. I felt at one with the universe, I felt that every cell in my body was alive and it was a very benevolent universe, wired for kindness.'

'It's when you get rid of your ego that you can see reality. Of course, it will always keep growing again, so you have to keep it trimmed back. The key to understanding how to deal with the problem is silence, because the ego always wants to keep on chattering.' Mike still believes that he has not yet experienced a real awakening, and is still determined to go to Japan.

I had no idea what to make of his – in many ways, bizarre – experience, but I did not feel inclined to argue with any of it. One question remained: why would an Englishman, from a feet-on-the-ground working-class background, pay good money to abase himself before an old, bald-headed Japanese man whom he had never seen before, and allow himself to be humiliated in that way?

'It was because of my absolute respect for him,' replied Mike, 'for his knowledge and his experience. He has an incredible presence. The other thing is that I have an intense desire to answer the fundamental questions of life and seek reality.'

'Zen teaches you that you will only see that reality when you rid yourself of your powerful, overbearing, controlling ego. When you manage to do that, it will change your life for ever.'

To adherents of Soto Zen, however, this passionate pursuit of awakenings that are extremely short-lived makes little or no sense. 'It's very childish, like running after a piece of candy', said Philippe

Coupey, a Zen master who lives in Paris. 'They get enlightenment and then they go home – but enlightenment doesn't just disappear like that.' In his view, it was hard to escape the feeling that the adherents of *rinzai* were engaged in a misguided and rather over-heated endeavour.

He also did not like the way that *rinzai*-style Zen gave people grades according to the number of *koans* they had been able to answer. 'For us,' he said, '*life* is a *koan*, a riddle, and we're not going to solve that!'

I told him about the somewhat grim intensity of the sitting I had stumbled into in North Oxford. 'When you're looking for something,' he said, 'that's what happens. Those people find themselves on a railway track and they don't want to fall off because they're going somewhere.' Coupey is the man to whom Rosemary looks for guidance.

He would not be everyone's idea of a Zen master, and could not be more different from my friend Mike's description of the abbot of the Japanese monastery. Coupey is American, he lives in an apartment, and mounted over the door of his living room is a Winchester saddle-gun. 'That', he said, 'is a part of my past.'

He has a wry appreciation of the realities of life. His father, who was very wealthy, had disinherited both him and his siblings. People with his father's life-style, remarked Coupey, tended to leave all their money to the last of their wives.

You didn't become a Zen master, he went on, it was others who saw you as such. Your authority depended on being accepted by them. But he had had to go to Japan – 'head office', as he put it – in order to be allowed to 'transmit' to his disciples, and clearly resented the fact.

He had been required to go to a seven-day *sesshin* in a Japanese monastery where you got up at two in the morning and did not go to bed until ten at night. He had, he said, been glad to get out of the place alive. All that to get a certificate, a piece of paper.

Coupey is unusual in other ways too. He is certainly no ra-ra evangelist. 'You have to decide what you want to do', he said. 'Are you trying to draw in people in large numbers or preach the virtues of quietness, or what?'

'My great master Deshimaru used to say that talking was fine, so long as it came out of silence and didn't come from egotistic desires and jealousies. Some like to teach and preach to others, but I don't do that. In most cases, I say to the people who come, "there is nothing to obtain here."'

Nevertheless, 200 or so people do come to the *dojo*, the room where he practises *zazen*. Perhaps 60 or 70 of them, he thinks, would reckon to be his disciples. That was not because of his teachings: he had his shortcomings; it was just because of the Soto tradition.

The practise was what mattered. 'You're sitting, in silence, in a body posture that changes your mind – with your back straight, head square on your shoulders, your hands and feet immobilised. That's extraordinary for your body. You're also doing other things for your mind.'

'First, you're looking at yourself and, in the beginning, you are disturbed by what you see. Then you get tired of being disturbed by what you see, meaning that you get tired of your own ego, your own baggage – and what is more boring than our own baggage?'

'The practise actually helps to dissolve the ego. Through it, people learn behaviour, how to be, how to hold themselves, how to give to others and not take for themselves. And you slowly cease to be as attached to the things in life which you were attached to before.'

'As you begin to go beyond ego, personal desire, our own little self, then you realise the importance of the practise, because the world has changed for you – the *dojo* has changed, the trees have changed, everything has changed – because you've changed.'

'It is very important, though, to sit together with others. If you sit alone, you begin to think you're someone special. That is dangerous. When you sit with others, you don't start to think you're stronger than other people. You realise you're like leaves on the same tree.'

As for silence, he did not regard it as golden. It was just there. 'Thinking, evolved people' felt it was so great that they hunted for it, but Coupey did not feel that way. He was not going to put up a barrier to noise, because noise was the way the world was.

'Look,' he said, 'I like silence, I like it physically because, in it, my brain is less rattled, but where it's really important is in the *dojo*. In the *dojo*, we have to come face to face with ourselves and not be disturbed by anything else.'

'Silence is a good way to confront the ego – in fact, from the ego point of view, it is an absolute necessity. And the time when you can really appreciate silence is when your own ego, your own wishes, are no longer in control.'

Coupey could scarcely live in more different circumstances than Dorji, a 25-year-old Tibetan monk who, when I met him in India, had just spent 10 months in a cave 11,000 feet up in the Himalayas.

He had already been a monk for four years when his master, Guru Kyab, instructed him to go to the cave. 'In our tradition,' said Dorji, 'on the path to enlightenment you have to undergo severe challenges or you will never know what spirituality means.'

The cave he was sent to was a place where a local shepherd used to keep his sheep when it was too cold for them to be outside. When Dorji arrived, he found the floor covered with sheep dung, but his master told him not to clear it away. He said Dorji would gain some richness from it, that it would save him. So Dorji simply covered the dung with grass and leaves.

All he took with him to the cave were a plate, a mug, a pot, a few kitchen implements and a simple mattress. His master brought him food each month. It was mostly roasted barley, the main staple of the Tibetan diet. There was no pleasure in eating such food, said Dorji, but it did keep you alive. Up there in the mountains, it snowed even in summer, sometimes for three or four days without stopping. If he felt ill, he had to run down the road to the nearest village, which was four kilometres away.

'I used to bring sandalwood for a fire,' he said, 'and pray to the local deities to ask for their help, and I would spend six hours each day in silent meditation. Whatever came to me in the silence which related to my spiritual journey I regarded as what you might call the voice of God.'

'For the first two or three months', he went on, 'I struggled a lot. Many times I felt I was going mad. I got frustrated and angry, I didn't know what I was trying to achieve. Sometimes I wrote poetry, which gave me great relief.'

'My master would come with instructions to help and inspire me but, when I asked if I could leave, I received scoldings from him. He said, "you cannot leave, this is the way and, if you do not want to stay in it, you can leave for ever." Deep down I really felt I was changing, so I accepted the challenge.'

'It is very hard to express the real meaning of enlightenment, but the aim is to achieve complete non-attachment, from not only all worldly things but divine things also. If you become attached even to divine things, then you become more egotistic, the feeling of being holy arises in your mind and that is a distraction from real spirituality.'

'Such a sense can give you a pleasant feeling of bliss, but then you get stuck there. It is really the same kind of pleasant feeling that you get from worldly attachments. Both are attachments. I can only measure my progress by the degree to which I can control my emotions. I often used to become angry at school and I was very restless in my teenage years.'

'For me, silence is the only answer, because it is only in silence that we can achieve non-attachment. Thoughts can never be stopped, and emotions, of course, come with them. If you cling to the thoughts, then you are putting yourself into the trap of attachment, which is the cause of all our suffering.'

'I am really happy with my spiritual journey and I shall go back to the cave soon because I felt very inspired by my months there. I really want to go back. I was emotionally a very weak person, so the cave is a challenge I have to undergo.'

For the vast majority of Buddhists, silence is clearly a time when they seek to banish thoughts rather than linger on them. Like Dorji, they want thoughts to come and then go. Some Tibetan Buddhists, however, including the Dalai Lama, speak about a kind of meditation during which they sit in silence and consider a particular issue.

Meditation of that kind was not easy, he said, when I spoke with him in Delhi. It had taken a year or two before he had become any good at it. Since then, he had been given much inspiration by the practise – thinking about other people, thinking of how to encourage the positive forces in the world and counteract the negative ones.

Anyway, that was his practise. He spent between four and five hours each day doing it, and then another hour before he went to bed. 'But', he added, 'most of my meditation is spent in sleep and I have eight or nine hours of uninterrupted sleep every night.' He chuckled, the chuckle of a much younger man. 'People are rather jealous of that!'

He is not the only prominent Buddhist who regards silence as much more than a time for clearing the mind. The Ajahn (abbot) of the Amaravati monastery 35 miles north-west of London is also in favour of sometimes using it in a way which is very close to a Christian notion of meditation.

Amaravati is perched on a low hill in the Hertfordshire countryside. Founded only in 1984, it is now a thriving establishment. There is a series of low buildings, neatly kept, a fine temple, a giant golden Buddha and 36 monks, nuns and novices. They follow the Theravada tradition – The Way of the Elders – which is typical of South Asian countries.

Outside the dining hall is a notice that says that the essence of Buddhism is 'to touch the place of truth in the heart through mindfulness'. The abbot, Amaro Bhikku, is an Englishman who has been a monk for 32 years. After boarding school in Kent, he took a degree in psychology and physiology at London University. Like his predecessor, an American called Sumedho, he has a striking openness and freedom from dogma.

Like Coupey, he has reservations about *rinzai* Zen's emphasis on 'great experiences of awakening. In Theravada,' he said, 'we wouldn't call it enlightenment, we might call it a powerful meditation experience. We wouldn't deny that it was totally valid, but we would believe that you can then get lost again. Yes, you may say, "I've seen, I've understood!," but we'd say "let's put the kettle on and talk about it."'

'Even if the experience is valid, the key is how it is understood. You may have seen ultimate reality, but there are still bits of self-delusion that can come back – the idea, for example, that "it's me who is enlightened, therefore I can do anything I like!" In the Theravada world, we would say "that's a wonderful experience but let's work at it, not grasp it so you get carried away by the memory of it, try to establish it in a more consistent and real fashion!"'

For him, he said, enlightenment meant a quality of complete peacefulness and freedom, when your heart and mind were perfectly attuned and responsive to each moment. He sounded for all the world like a middle-of-the-road Anglican vicar warning the born-again against the dangers of over-enthusiasm.

In the life of his own monastery, Bhikku went on, silence was at the heart of everything. During the three months of their winter retreat, they practised what they called noble silence, which meant only speaking to each other in case of real need. Each day during that time, they spent eight or nine hours in formal group meditation, and those times, of course, were held in total silence. They did not, he added, make use of the stick like the practitioners of Zen.

Stilling the tongue had great value in itself. He had once talked with a Trappistine nun who had said that theirs had seemed like a harmonious community until they had started speaking. When that happened, she had told him, all kinds of things came out. They had discovered, for example, that some of the Sisters had very strange ideas about the nature of the Christian life!

There was, though, another and more important kind of silence – internal silence. Your mouth might be quiet, but your mind was still carrying on an unrelenting dialogue. The Buddha, said the abbot, had been afraid that the idea of silence would become a fetish, that his followers would mistake the external form of the practise for its real purpose, and still remain very noisy inside.

So, while stilling one's speech was important, at a more radical level it was crucial to find silence both from one's habitual attitudes and from one's emotions – feelings of self-concern, irritation, restlessness and annoyance – because those mental agitations created a level of noise inside you.

Was silence, then, a journey into mental nothingness? 'Not at all', replied Bhikku. 'It's a vehicle to help us on a journey towards freedom and perfect peace. It supports the qualities of calm and insight into yourself and other people. It creates a clearer backdrop against which thoughts and feelings and perceptions can be discerned.'

'It is true', he went on, 'that the majority of Buddhists would regard silent meditation as a way of bringing the mind to thought-free quietness, but you don't need the mind to be completely free of thought to be peaceful and, as we see it, silence can also be used for what we call wise reflection.'

That did not just mean calculating the pros and cons of a situation or problem but, first of all, finding as much quietude as you could and then introducing into your mind for reflection a single question about something that was worrying you – and asking what you should do about it.

'It's very important', he said, 'that you should not load the question when you ask it of yourself. You should approach it in as unbiased a way as possible, try to clear away the clutter of your habitual attitudes and then see what arises.'

'It might be like hearing a thought that is not in your own voice. What a Christian might call the voice of God or an interior locution, but what we think of as our intuitive wisdom. In the silence, you are inviting that wisdom to come to the surface. It comes from somewhere within, it's an intrinsic quality of the heart and mind.'

He gave a couple of examples. 'You are married but there is another woman in the picture. As you reflect on it all, there is the voice which says "my marriage is really over, my wife is pretty boring and she'd really be quite OK about this anyway."'

'Then there's the other voice which says "that's all rubbish!" So you're learning to listen to the voices which chatter in your mind, you're following the argument, and then there is a genuine intuition which comes from pure wisdom and in the clearest terms – "what you're doing is deceitful and unworthy behaviour!" When you are able to discern that intuition, you should follow it through because you cannot fool reality.'

'Or take a case where you are feeling deep regret about something that has happened. For example, there is the story of the woman who took her niece and several other children to the beach. She was not paying attention and one of them got swept away and died. Not surprisingly, she spent countless hours beating herself up about it.

'So how would wise reflection have helped her – or you if you were feeling the same kind of regret about something? You'd look at your feeling of regret or guilt, be as honest with yourself as you could, and ask yourself how culpable you really were.'

'You'd probably hear the voice which said "you're the rottenest person ever, you'll never be forgiven," and the other voice which says "it wasn't all your fault." Then you might come to a sense of repentance and admit that it *was* your fault, but use the pain and grief to decide to be more mindful and caring in future. You could use the energy of pain, not swallowing it as an eternal crime, but not dismissing it as insignificant either.'

Wise reflection, said Bhikku, could be such a help in clearing a space in our minds so that we could hear that inner voice, and give us the sense of perspective that flowed from our intuitive wisdom. We needed the help of that wisdom which could come, in silence, from within us. Which sounded, to the non-Buddhist, like nothing so much as giving the voice of conscience a chance.

14

The prisoner's tale

Silence is very hard to come by in prison, as any inmate will tell you. Outside jail, noise can be irritating, even tormenting. Inside, in those cramped and claustrophobic spaces, with prisoners spending as much as 19 hours in their cells every day, it can be literally maddening, a pressure-cooker of seemingly endless tumult.

'It is a hell from which silence has been banished', said John, a prisoner who was accustomed to go on silent retreats when he was a free man. 'Buildings of brick that echo and amplify every whisper, no soft furnishings here; the clanking and clanging of barred steel gates being opened and closed; warders shouting orders and with their personal intercoms continually operating, televisions, radios and CDs blaring inconsiderately down corridors, alarm bells ringing …'

'During the day', said Ian Sutherland, who is doing life for murder in a Scottish jail, 'one of the greatest disturbances is dance music – boom!, boom!, boom! for six hours without stopping just a couple of cells away.'

'Then there are doors banging, keys jangling, staff shouting people's names at the tops of their voices, riot alarm bells going off when a fight breaks out. If you can imagine an underpass, with kids kicking tins around and shouting all the time, that's what it's like. Even at two in the morning, conventional silence simply does not exist.'

As if this cacophony were not enough, there are also prisoners desperately seeking to assuage their guilt and unhappiness in torrents of words. 'Whether they are guilty or not,' said a young Englishman whom I met in an American jail, 'they are always eager, often from the moment when they meet you, to tell you about all the lies that have been told about them. They never shut up.'

'They want to be seen as victims of the system and they can only do that by talking until their audience relents and appears to accept their version of the story. And if they can't convince you of their victim status, they'll try to show you that at least they're not as bad as other people in the jail. "Well, at least I didn't ..." or "at least I'm not ...," they'll say. Both guilt and innocence drive their incessant talk.'

How, then, in this constant turmoil of noise, can there possibly be any chance for prisoners to discover the benefits which silence may have to offer? There are admirable organisations, such as the Prison Phoenix Trust in Britain, which correspond regularly with prisoners and encourage them to practise meditation and yoga. They do so in the hope that either or both will not only give them respite from the racket but also promote spiritual growth. Given the circumstances, though, that might sound like a lost cause.

Yet the Trust reckons that about 4,000 prisoners have taken up their offer and practise either meditation or yoga, sometimes both, often with qualified teachers. Some of the 4,000 are, on the face of things, the most unlikely people to be doing anything of the kind. Yet, when you meet them, listen to their stories and even read their diaries, there is no denying that silent meditation has changed their horribly trammelled lives in the most remarkable way.

Ian Sutherland, who was 40 when I met him, is in prison at Glenochil, a bleak and barren spot in central Scotland, but with a line of low hills in the middle distance. It was not easy to get permission to see him. Only an intervention by the Phoenix Trust persuaded the prison governor to give me leave to pay him a visit.

Going into the prison, I was immediately aware that I was entering a place from which all liberty has been banished. I was told I could only take cash with me into the jail. I then made the mistake of asking if I might take a single sheet of paper with me. It had on it nothing more than the questions I intended to ask Sutherland. None the less the request aroused suspicion and was refused.

Why was I coming, one of the security guards wanted to know. For a moment, it looked as if I would not be allowed in at all. Only by producing the letter from the governor was I able to save the day and join the other visitors.

There were 60 or 70 of us that afternoon and we were all escorted into the spacious Visit Room. At the appointed hour, the prisoners filed in, all of them dressed in red shirts and blue trousers. Sutherland spotted me, though we had never met before, and came over hand outstretched. He was thin-faced and intense, but smiling. He is prisoner number 32643.

This, as he had already told me in letters, was a man who had killed someone who was supposed to be a friend and then carved up his body into little pieces with a handsaw to try to dispose of it. I could not help, as I looked at him, thinking of the ghastly event that had brought him to this place. I had never met anyone like that before.

Might I, I asked, ask him any question? 'Anything at all', he replied. He struck me immediately as someone who had nothing to hide. He makes no attempt to deny that he killed a man and added, for good measure, that if he had been caught for all that he had done he would be doing 200 years in Glenochil.

He does believe, however, that he should have been charged not with murder but with culpable homicide, given that the 'friend' he killed had kept on making homosexual advances to him and that he himself was high on drink and drugs at the time. At the moment, he is trying to persuade the Scottish Court of Appeal to review his case.

He is perfectly candid about his past life. 'I'm coming', he said, 'from a background of total hedonism. Everything was excess – sex in excess, drugs in excess, drink in excess. There was 20 years of that from the time when I was 16.'

He did not want to offer it as any sort of excuse but, as the only child of his mother's second marriage, he had never felt wanted. His parents had met his basic needs, but that was all. He had had two accidents as a child, in one of which his leg had been broken. By the time he went back to school, he had felt alone and 'thick', so he had stopped going.

By now beyond his parents' control, he was sent to a children's home, where the treatment was often brutal. When he kept on wetting his bed, one of the staff had simply bashed his head against the wall. He never wet the bed again.

During these years, so far as he could remember, his parents had never visited him. His father had left home when he was 12 and he had only seen him three times in the next 28 years. When I saw him in Glenochil, he was not expecting any other visitor during that year.

He did not mind that, he insisted, 'because it's not nice for them to have to come to a place like this.'

'My best years', he added poignantly, 'were between the ages of 18 months and three years. I had a little tractor, but then Mum and Dad sold it and life was never the same again.'

By the time he was in his 20s, Sutherland had become a persistent offender and for ever more serious crimes – breaching the peace, assault, rape – and had become a sort of prison tourist, sampling a whole series of Scottish jails: Edinburgh, Dumfries, Peterhead, until he came, at last, to Glenochil in 2010.

In the jail at Dumfries, however, Sutherland's life had slowly begun to take a different turn. In 2005 he had picked up a book entitled *We're All Doing Time*. 'In the book,' he said, 'the author kept on mentioning this chap called the Buddha, who talked about getting in touch with who you really were, and that rang a bit of a bell.'

'I'd had a Catholic upbringing and I resented it. It was all very strict, like the Inquisition. Their approach was "don't ask any questions, just believe!" and, when I got to the stage where I could think for myself, I disregarded it. My philosophy became "you live, you die, so have a good time in between."'

'Buddha's advice, from what I could gather, seemed to be "don't believe anything I tell you, don't believe in religion or spiritual teachers, don't believe just because it's been written down somewhere – but if, after investigating, you find something beneficial in this, do your best to live up to it."'

'I thought "hang on, if that's religion he's talking about, what happened to the other kind?: you *will*, you *will*, you *will*."' There didn't seem to be any dogma in this. That intrigued me. The religion

I had known was a set of rules and regulations and yet here was a guy who was saying "there are no rules, regulations or dogmas, just something to take a look at." '

'And it left you free to decide. Fantastic if you found something in it but no great drama if you didn't. Never in my life had I come across anything where you weren't told to do something – and there was nobody involved who claimed to have a monopoly on the Heaven-or-Hell situation.'

'So I went to the education department to ask whether they had any books on the Buddha. I was a wee bit embarrassed, because I thought they'll be imagining that I'd got religion, all that born-again stuff, I'm a new man and so on. The education coordinator did look at me with what I thought was disdain, though that may be putting it too strongly, but he said "leave it to me." '

'When I went back to the English class I'd been taking, this wee book on the Buddha turned up. The English teacher, Carol, said aloud in the class, "What were you asking about the Buddha for?" and that was even more embarrassing. But then she said "There's a Buddhist community just down the road from here. It's called Samye Ling and I'll give you their address." '

'Now at this point', Sutherland went on, 'I was still smoking, still taking drugs. There's plenty of that stuff in prison – heroin, hash and so on. So it was dope, cigarettes, just a continuation of my outside life. And I was very angry at the world, because I thought everyone else was to blame for what had happened to me.'

Thus began a journey which, with many doubts, hesitations and backward glances, has given new hope and purpose to a man who had had precious little of either.

In the interminable din of prison, Sutherland has set out to find a different way of living; to discover, through meditation, an inner silence, an inner peace that will help him leave behind the utterly self-destructive life that he had been leading for decades. As he says himself, it is the bravest thing he has ever tried to do.

He wrote to the Tibetan Buddhists at Samye Ling. A German called Max came to see him, they discussed meditation, and Sutherland decided to set aside 20 minutes each day for it. Within a month, he had stopped smoking and taking drugs. He had also, for reasons he did not fully understand himself, taken a vow never to spit again and to stop swearing.

At the same time, a real battle was going on inside him. 'One part of my mind was saying "give this up, it's a waste of time," another part was saying "you must stick with it."'

'In those first few months, I was asking myself what was going on. I was expecting peace and tranquillity, the heavens to open – but none of that was taking place. One morning I'd say to myself "I'm not going on doing this," but, ten minutes later, I had started meditating again. It was as if a nice comforting voice inside me was saying "this is what you need."'

'The other problem was that, in trying to meditate in silence, I had suddenly become aware of all the racket. When I'd arrived in prison, I'd paid no attention to the noise. At that time, I had no spiritual side, so it didn't bother me. Now I started hearing things much more violently – doors banging, people shouting all the time.'

'I made the mistake of trying to find peace in conventional silence, and that sort of silence is something that just doesn't exist in prison.

It's a mistake I still make, because my mind isn't settled enough. I'm not a good enough practitioner.'

'Much later, when I'd been moved to Peterhead, I thought I'd get up at four in the morning to find some real silence, but then I discovered there was a seagull nooky factory outside the window and you could hear all those crazy noises they make while they're mating.' It made him feel all the more strongly that he was trying to swim upstream.

After a few months of trying – and failing – to learn how to meditate, help arrived in an unexpected guise.

A Buddhist nun, an older Scottish lady known as the Venerable Mary, began to come to visit Sutherland in Dumfries to help and encourage him. She was, he recalls, dressed in burgundy-coloured robes with a yellow sash. She came to see him as many as seven times in a single year.

He complained to Mary that his mind had become busier, not quieter, that he had begun to ponder the events of his past life and to try to plan how he wanted the future to be. Far from criticising him, Mary told him that that was all good because he was becoming more aware of the movements of his mind, and that he must continue with meditation.

Too many people, she said, gave up on Buddhism just when they were beginning to get somewhere. Sutherland kept going partly because he did not want to disappoint Mary, since she was coming so far to see him.

At the same time, he was conscious that something positive was happening inside him. 'The ego is mighty,' he said, 'but I had a sense of what Buddhists would call my inner self beginning to come to the surface, like a light shining through a window – and in these circumstances the ego feels terribly threatened.'

'All that inner conflict plays horrid tricks on you – anxieties, hypochondria, imagining that you've got illnesses you don't really have. I was beginning to see other people in a different light but the ego kept on telling me "you're an idiot doing all this!"'

'I think the inner being I'm speaking of is the ability always to do the right thing, to do what is virtuous, hopefully for the benefit of other people as well as yourself. It is a very arduous undertaking.'

'The best way I can explain what I was trying to do in silent meditation is this. The sun, which is our inner being, our true self, is always shining but, for the moment, there may be clouds covering it. When you meditate, you start to brush those clouds away.'

'When they are brushed away, you start to get in touch with your true self. An Anglican monk once said that, in order to find your true self, you might have to go through terrifying experiences. It's like facing your old self and presenting it with a different option.'

'It's like a war going on, and it's going on even now. Every day is a battle. Sometimes the ego wins, sometimes my inner self. It happens on a moment by moment basis. A few times I've almost thrown in the towel.'

'I was trying hard to change my behaviour towards people, but I found it very difficult. The further along the path I went, the more difficult the people I came up against seemed to be. I'd ask a member of the prison staff if he could book me a visit and he'd say "no, I'm not allowing that." And I was thinking, "I changed my ways, surely the world should be changing with me". By this time, Sutherland's fellow inmates had nicknamed him Buddha.'

The daily struggle within Sutherland is plain to see in the diary that he began to keep after arriving at Glenochil. It reveals a man battling against all the irritations of prison life, the torment of having forfeited his freedom, sometimes sunk in despair but always, somehow, struggling back to the surface, trying to keep the vows he has made, intensely self-critical about his failures, clinging to the new way of life he has found.

1   December 1st, 2010: 'I have seen enough violence to last me the rest of my life. When I started to study the teaching of the Buddha over five years ago, I made a vow not to hurt anyone ever again. I have found it very difficult at times to keep to that in here, but as yet I have not lashed out in violence. I have not been so restrained with my mouth or mind, sadly.'

2   December 2nd: 'Everything is now covered with snow. I really love the snow, must be the child in me. Had I behaved … better in life then maybe I could have been out playing in the snow with Mirin (his daughter). Maybe not … as she will be 12 years old now. I do really hope that one day I will get to see her again. It has been eight years since I last saw her.'

3   December 6th: 'I don't judge anyone, I do my best to take people as I find them no matter their past. When that door bangs shut at night it's a big enough job dealing with your own regret without adding to someone else's pain … As I have found, the hardest person to forgive is one's self.'

With all his ups and downs, though, what had been the value thus far of all the hours of silent meditation? 'The first thing', replied Sutherland, 'is that I now accept that what's happened in my life is down to me and nobody else. That even stretches to things outwith my control. When things happen now, it's because of my past actions in this life or previous incarnations.'

'That is such a big relief to me. Before, I could blame everything on other people – my mother didn't love me enough and so on. It was always his fault, their fault. It's a relief in the sense that I no longer carry that anger, that angst on my soul, as if you always felt you'd been done wrong by the world. I was always pointing and blaming, and with all that anger there has to be a big waste of energy.'

'The second thing is that I now know that there is a purpose to my life, which is to be the best possible human being I can be, and to treat everyone as I would want to be treated myself.'

'The third thing is that I am a completely different person than the man who walked through that prison door. You could say, in a way, that I'm a prison monk. I'm a terrible practitioner of Buddhism, but I'm consistent and I try my best. It's the only thing I've never given up on. I've often almost thrown in the towel, but something always pulls me back. I can't tell you what it is.'

How, though, did he manage to cope with all the things he had done? 'In the beginning,' said Sutherland, 'I just pushed it to the back of my mind. Then Buddhism helped me to handle what took place. It says that the past has been and gone, there is no point dwelling on it.'

'I don't want to be bland and say it doesn't matter, because, of course, it does. It was a very horrid thing that took place, particularly since Alan was a friend, but it wouldn't have happened if I hadn't been in the state of mind produced by the life I'd lived over the previous 20 years. A volcano erupts every now and then and that's what happened to me. I was a powder keg.'

'What I did to Alan is as clear as the day I did it, and that is going to be there for ever. I can see the body of someone who was seriously kind to me, I can see every cut that I made. He had made a sexual advance to me and I snapped.'

'So yes, it is still a burden to me, but there is no word in Tibetan Buddhism for guilt, they don't understand the term. They speak about regret, and the beauty of regret is that you can have resolve and, if you have resolve, you can have the remedy, you can alleviate the suffering.'

'It doesn't mean I forget it, become blasé. It means that I understand why it happened and that I've vowed never to do anything like it again. Not only did I vow not to do those things, I also vowed never to eat meat or any living thing again. I've been doing that for six years now.'

'When I'm out in the exercise yard and it's been raining, there are all the little worms. People are squashing them by accident, but I pick them up knowing what I've done in the past, knowing what being silent in meditation has taught me. I'm trying my best not to harm any living creature, however small. That's the regret, that's the resolve, that's the remedy.'

'Because of what's happened to me, I can try to be the best human being I can possibly be and automatically qualify for forgiveness. If I went back to my old ways, it would be an insult to Alan's death, and a slap in the face to all the people I've hurt and, believe me, I have caused a lot of problems for people.'

'But this has to be the most difficult place to study the spiritual life. You're faced with a constant barrage of insensitive and angry people. There is no let-up. I have the image of trying to climb Everest – and the further up the mountain you go, the more arduous it becomes. I'd never have kept going if I hadn't had the support of the Prison Phoenix Trust.'

'I sometimes ask myself how my meditation can be of benefit to me when I still get irate with people, when I'm still full of lust, hatred, jealousy and pride, sometimes almost worse than it was in the beginning.'

'But with it there are also beautiful moments of peace, understanding and enrichment. I'm facing up to things for the first time. I've lied all my life, but now I'm learning to be truthful. And what was once just a wee spark has now become a flame. Yes, that flame gets blown about, but it never goes out.'

'I do get lonely because I don't have regular contact with a Buddhist teacher, so I've had to try to become my own guru, using my very limited understanding to create a practise that suits my needs. I do an hour's meditation a day, though not every day, and at the moment I'm concentrating on Zen meditation, using a mantra.'

'The mind stops, all thought ceases and you're at one with God or the Great Spirit or the Buddha. I do it because of what comes out of the silence – peace, love, understanding.'

'Buddha says that all of us on earth are trying to get home – which you can call heaven, nirvana, paradise, it's all the same thing. It's like the seed which lies within us. All we can do with that seed is plant it, water it, perhaps put a fence around it. For the rest, we have to rely on grace – and that is what meditation can help you find.'

'Prisons, you know, are not created by bricks and mortar, by locked doors. They are built within people's hearts and minds. It is only there that all of us will find freedom. My prison ended when I came to prison, because I was in a worse prison outside.'

'If I was lying on my deathbed moments from death and the Dalai Lama came in and said "this Buddhist stuff is a load of rubbish," do you know what I'd do? I'd say "I don't care, it is the best thing I have ever done in my life!"'

In the months since we met, Sutherland and I have regularly exchanged letters. His are always honest but they are never, ever depressing. On the contrary, they are full of an underlying cheerfulness even though, on present form, he cannot apply for parole until 2021.

He is obviously reading widely. He quotes Jesus, the Buddha and writers such as Thomas Merton. He presses me to read books that he believes will be of help to me. He sent me a delightful, home-made Christmas card with Merton's advice: 'so keep still and let Him do his work. This is what it means to renounce not only pleasure and possessions but even your own self.'

In one of his letters he told me that he had written to his mother, to assure her that the fact that he had ended up in prison did not have anything at all to do with her, that she had always done her best for him. That, he said, had 'gone down a storm', though she had not yet been to see him.

The 'wee flame' clearly has not gone out. 'If I ever get out of here,' he told me, 'and I found myself living in a cardboard box, totally destitute, I would still find time to be in touch with who I really am, to help me find my way home.'

15

Desert fathers

The monastery of St Macarius the Great, which was founded more than 1,600 years ago, could easily be mistaken for a prison or a fortress. Its massive ramparts tower up out of the Egyptian countryside just a few miles off the highway from Cairo to Alexandria. It looks more like a bastion to repel intruders than a place of religious devotion.

The walls of its great circular citadel have many small windows but only one modest, narrow entrance for visitors. Beyond it, the dunes of the Western Desert stretch all the way to the Libyan border. When we arrived, a man was sweeping the ever-encroaching sand away from the door.

Once inside, the welcome was warm. I was clearly expected. The American chaplain to the Anglican Bishop of Cairo, who had driven me there, made the introductions. The monks – Coptic Christians – who seemed inordinately cheerful, were all dressed in the most striking black robes and head-dresses.

The head-dresses are woven with thirteen gold crosses, six on either side of a golden dividing band which runs down the centre of the head, and with the thirteenth cross at the back. The golden band, as I discovered later, is a symbol of the way in which St Anthony, who founded the first desert monastery in Egypt in the fourth century, felt that his head was being split asunder by his battle against the temptations of the Devil.

Twelve of the crosses represent the Apostles, the thirteenth Christ himself. They are all intended to protect the desert fathers from any evil thinking. The head-dress also has a tail, a symbol of the fact that its wearer has now left the world behind. Beneath their gowns, the monks wear a leather belt marked with three crosses to help them preserve their chastity.

I was shown to my quarters, which were adequate, if a touch penitential. My bedroom, on the second floor, was at the end of a long, rather dusty corridor and had a zero on the door, perhaps to give me a sense of my own nothingness. A sizeable number of hungry mosquitoes were already in residence.

The eating arrangements were scarcely more inviting. The dining table was in an area that was dusty, dark and dismal. There was neither a plate, nor any cutlery or crockery worth the name. Food arrived daily in a tier of steel containers. The first day's supply, for example, consisted of three hard-boiled eggs, some tasteless yoghurt and some extremely salty, home-made cheese. I always ate alone, with only the mosquitoes for company.

Despite these unpromising circumstances, the next three days were among the most enriching of my life. I came to love the monastery and the monks. The whole experience left an indelible mark on me.

After a somewhat desultory supper, a monk appeared who was to be my guide and counsellor during the next days. His name was Abouna – Father – Mercurius. We became friends effortlessly and, as we talked in the gathering gloom, fought a largely futile battle against the mosquitoes.

With a good deal of laughter, we competed to see how many of the wily creatures we could account for. They won the battle hands down. We only managed to kill one each.

Mercurius told me that he was 39 and that, until he became a monk 15 years ago, he had been an architect. He'd been only too happy to leave all that behind, but his mother and father had both wept bitterly when he told them of his intention. Now they come to see him three times each year, but still feel that they have lost their only son.

Had his time at St Macarius been a happy one, though? 'Very, very happy', replied Mercurius. Was that because he was a good man? 'No,' he replied, 'I'm not a good man, but maybe this is the right place for me.' Mercurius's devoutness is worn lightly. He is like someone who has simply surrendered to sunlight and does not need to make a great fuss about it.

He'd chosen to become a desert father, he said, because he wanted to be with God in this place, and in Egypt 80 per cent of their saints had been desert monks. The desert was a very good place to cleanse you heart and have a quiet time with God. All the 130 monks at St Macarius would, he was sure, agree with that. They all experienced the desert as a space where they could meet God.

'From the first day we enter here,' said Mercurius, 'we are in silence for a great deal of the time. The main exception is when we are working together in the fields, where words are necessary. We have a saying, "shut down your mouth to let your heart talk and then shut down your heart to let God speak." So it is lips, heart, God. If we don't speak in our hearts with God, then silence is nothing.'

Did he and the other monks really feel that God did somehow communicate with them in the silence? 'Of course', he replied, as though it was the most foolish of questions. 'In our hearts every day, in every prayer, in every reading of the Bible.'

'In my experience, it brings peace, you feel your heart to be full of love – and sometimes, though rarely, the communication comes in the form of words. It is not like someone speaking but it comes into our hearts – "do this, do that, take care of this man, that situation." They are thoughts from elsewhere, not from ourselves.'

He gave me an example. 'I was very busy with the work in the fields, in our banana and mango plantations, and every day I came back to my cell utterly exhausted. We have a local phone network just for the monastery which we can use freely with no charge, and I was making calls every evening to prepare the work for the next day.'

'Then, one day, in a time of silence, I heard a very clear voice which said "don't worry too much about all this dust, remember why you came here!" That meant that the work might be good work but caring about it more than my eternal life was the wrong way to go.'

'I felt shocked when I heard His voice. It wasn't that I had been searching for it. It came suddenly completely out of the blue. "Leave this dust, remember why you came to this life!" '

'So I asked myself again why I had become a monk – was it really to worry about all the work in the fields? I spent the next seven days in a state of wonder and then I decided to spend less time in the fields. I also finished with all those phone calls.'

'It was the turning point in my life here. That thought was

absolutely not from myself because I cared such a lot about the work in the fields. The trouble was that I had become too deeply involved in it.'

There had been other occasions when he had heard a very clear voice that seemed to come from elsewhere. He had wanted a particular man to work with him in the fields, a man with a lot of skill and energy. He had asked God for His opinion and the thought came clearly: 'don't ask this man to come and work with you'; and he had obeyed.

Three or four days later, he had realised that, if he had not obeyed, it would have brought him many problems. He did not tell me why, but said that he had thanked God with all his heart.

The monastery, he went on, owned a 3,000-acre estate and, on the 60 per cent that they cultivated, they grew olives, dates, fruits such as oranges, bananas and mangoes, as well as almost all their own vegetables. They also had a chicken farm, two farms with cows and a fish farm. The income made them comfortably self-sufficient, and they used the surplus to help poor families from Upper Egypt. They employed about 800 workers from that area during the summer months.

On the perimeter of the estate, Mercurius added, they had four or five hermits who spent their whole lives in almost complete silence. Some were in places three or four kilometres away from the monastery, they didn't work in the fields, they had no mobile phones (unlike most of the monks) and they practised silence throughout the day.

They came to Mass twice each month, but took no part in daily prayer and meals and had no electricity in their hermitages. Would it, I asked, be possible to meet one of these hermits? Mercurius was silent for a long time. 'I will think about it', he said.

Then we both retired from our battle with the mosquitoes, and Mercurius prepared to leave me. There was just one thing, he added. I should not under any circumstances go walking in the desert. There were serpents and wolves out there, it was dangerous.

The next morning, in glorious sunshine, I walked down the road from the monastery to look at one of their cattle farms, and saw dozens of contented, healthy-looking beasts. On the way back, I came upon an old desert father sitting by the side of the road. He told me that he had been a monk for 39 years and had first come to St Macarius while he was still studying for his master's degree in pharmacy.

One day, when he had already been at the monastery for many years, he had been feeling very tired and heavy in spirit. Then, quite suddenly, he had heard Jesus say 'don't you want to suffer with me a little?' – and immediately his condition had changed and he had become very happy.

'It was something like a miracle', he said. 'His voice is very sweet and comfortable to the soul. You can't compare it with any other voice. He doesn't talk very much, and it depends on him when he speaks to you.'

He had had another wonderful experience, he went on. 'I saw, in the twinkling of an eye, a vision of the Kingdom of God – and it was very beautiful, very luminous and full of peace. I am a great sinner and my only hope is to be cleansed by the blood of Jesus Christ, but please tell your readers that it is present, it is here, it is real. I felt that a gift like that experience was equal to the whole of life.' Could it, I wondered, have been a Christian version of the Zen experience of enlightenment?

Then the old monk spoke about the man, Father Matta-el-Meskeen – Matthew the Poor – who had been sent by the Coptic Pope to restore the monastery in 1969 at a time when it was close to collapse. Matta had found all the buildings in a very bad condition and there were only six old monks left – but over the next 30 years he had completely transformed the place. 'Matta', said the old monk, 'had a very big vision, not like my little one.'

When I got back to the monastery, I found Mercurius waiting for me. He had, he said, no idea whether any of the hermits would be willing to talk to me, but we could at least go and ask them.

So we set off down the dusty perimeter track of the monastery's estate. It was boiling hot. I told Mercurius about Noël Coward's song, 'Mad Dogs and Englishmen'. He laughed. 'Now there are two mad dogs', he said, 'you and me.'

We came first to a simple, stone-built hermitage in the shadow of the sand dunes. Mercurius went ahead to see if the hermit felt inclined to see me. I waited concealed behind a hedge to spare the poor man the embarrassment of refusing me to my face.

In fact, Father Phillipus came out and greeted me warmly but said that, sadly, he felt unable to answer my questions. I quite understood. After all, I was intruding on a profound silence. So on we went and, after another half-mile or so, came to another hermitage.

This time the answer was positive. Father D was quite happy to talk and would try to answer all my questions, said Mercurius, but had asked if he might remain anonymous. This desert father was still 'going through struggles', he said.

There was no sign of them when we met. Father D seemed entirely at peace. He was a vigorous, cheerful man of 39 with a black beard and black eyes. He welcomed us into his sun-filled hermitage which, surprisingly, has a small sitting room, a bedroom, a bathroom and a kitchenette, all very luxurious by the standards of the original desert fathers but still relatively simple.

In the sitting room there was a small carpet and a couple of chairs. On the walls were images of Christ, the Virgin Mary, the Archangel Michael, St Anthony and St Paul.

From the moment when we began talking, I felt that Father D's answers came from a deep well of silence, from a man who had stripped himself of almost all human contact, who had looked deep inside himself and had stood naked before the God whom he regarded as his maker and redeemer. His answers were entirely unvarnished and betrayed no desire either to please or convince me.

Before he had become a monk in the year 2000, he said, he had been running a factory which made bricks. That had now been taken over by his younger brother. Then, in 2008, he had persuaded his fellow monks, against some resistance from the older brethren, to allow him to live this life of silence and solitude. It had clearly been something of a battle, but they had eventually yielded in the face of Father D's passionate desire to be given what he regarded as freedom.

Now, he said, he saw only one other human being for perhaps 15 minutes each week, when one of his fellow-monks brought his supply of food and drink. He also went to Mass once a month and would then often stay the previous night in the monastery.

Why, I asked, had he chosen this life of solitude and silence, the deep, pregnant silence of the desert? 'To get close to God', he replied, 'and to have time for deep meditation. The man who loves his wife and hopes to spend the rest of his life with her wants to be alone in a quiet place with her during their honeymoon.' So it was with him and Christ.

How, then, did he spend his day? 'With Jesus,' Father D replied, 'and without any limitations. I take half an hour's walk each day for the sake of exercise, but the monk who lives alone wants to go, step by step, deeper into prayer until he is praying the whole night long.'

'Our forefathers in the desert did that, and that is what I am going to do. At the moment, I go to bed at eight, rise again at one in the morning and then spend the rest of the night in prayer until the sun rises.' For a man who had been up for most of the night, he showed no sign of tiredness.

'One of the great virtues of silence', he went on, 'is that it helps you see things as they really are, stripping away their deceptive outer appearances. The things which capture your mind out in the world suddenly seem false despite all their glitter.'

'Man is created with two natures – the nature of flesh, with all its passion for eating, drinking, sleeping and all the rest – and then the nature of spirit. Here in this lonely place there is time to feed that spirit.'

'When you are with Jesus, there is a feeling of absolute peace, absolute quietness and absolute joy. When you are with him, you have no feeling of struggle between your two natures.'

Father D said all this without the faintest tinge of piosity. It was, to him, a simple statement of fact, of daily experience, a statement that came from a man who knows the bliss of a personal relationship with Jesus which millions of Christians yearn for but never find. It seemed utterly irrelevant to ask him if he were a happy man. He has plainly experienced something beyond mere happiness.

I wondered, though, if he ever felt lonely? 'If a man's relationship with God is weak,' he replied, 'he may feel lonely. I have very rarely felt like that, though God does let it happen from time to time just to make me humble again. To know, too, what it is like to be one of those people who are separated from God, so that I can really feel for them and pray for them.'

There were, I said, people with strong Christian beliefs who felt that men such as himself, who had left the world to give their whole lives to God, were in a sense carrying the rest of us on their backs, acting as our advocates at the Throne of Heavenly Grace, as they would put it. There were, however, also others, many of them, who believed that the life he was leading was a complete waste of time, that he should get out into the world and start doing something useful. Many of them were good and decent people. How did he respond to criticism of that kind?

Father D was not inclined to be in any way defensive. There were, he said, so many benefits that flowed from a monk being in a remote place such as this where his only work was prayer. He was not praying only for himself, but for the salvation of the whole world.

God had rightly said that, if there were only ten just men in the life of a city, He would forgive that city for all its failings. Nor did the monk who lived alone have the least sense of apartness. On the contrary, he felt very deeply the trials of those who lived out in the world.

It was, in truth, a rather standard answer and the rational mind may find such logic – if, indeed, it is logic – wholly unacceptable. But then Father D sees things through different eyes than the rest of us, and who can be sure that he is wrong?

He had chosen, I said, to spend his life in almost total silence, but if silence were so marvellous, why did so many people instinctively shrink away from it? Father D's answer was blunt. 'It is sin', he said, 'which makes a man not want to be alone in silence. It makes him want to do anything but that, because silence strips a man naked. Satan wants a man to do anything but be silent. There are people who do many good things but they still avoid silence at all costs.'

'Silence for such people can seem very dangerous, but then, sometimes, there can come a certain whisper in their minds. It can start with a few seconds of quiet and then it becomes a few minutes, and when they eventually taste the joyfulness of silence – after a few days in the desert, you can actually taste the silence, not by nose or mouth but in the heart – it encourages them to enter it again and again.'

'You find everything in this world except silence', he went on. 'If a man draws everything of this world to himself, he still feels inside that there is something else he wants – and, until he finds that thing, he will not be satisfied. A man may not even know what it is – the Devil blinds his eyes to it – but he can find that something through silence.'

That was talk enough. When we left, Father D walked a little way along the track with us. I suggested to Mercurius that he should tell the hermit about Noël Coward's song. Mercurius was reluctant, feeling perhaps that it was inappropriate after such privileged moments, but he soon relented.

Father D was convulsed with laughter. 'Now', he said, 'there are three mad dogs!' He may lead a solitary life, but he does not take himself too seriously and he does not suffer from the sin of worthiness.

That was just one of many memorable encounters at St Macarius. During those next days, seven or eight of the monks poured out for me the riches of their experience of the desert and its – for them – fruitful silence.

They were, to a man, full of peace and a kind of quiet joy. There was no otiose piety, no fervent declarations of having been born again, just a profound humility – and honesty about the fact that they had not come to their present state without pain and suffering. They had clearly paid, and were still paying, the price in self-surrender for their peace of heart. They had all been salted by the fire of the discipline.

Father Shishoy is a former surveyor who had been a hermit for ten years and only came back to the monastery because he was asked to take charge of its 14 novices. 'When I first went off into the desert to live alone,' he said, 'I walked a few metres and then I wanted to take off and fly. There was an explosion of joy in my heart. I actually shouted for joy, I couldn't hold it back. Freedom, I thought!'

Those early days in the desert had been wonderful. Sometimes he had actually jumped for joy, but then came the hard times. 'It was like struggles with the Devil', he said. 'Sometimes there was loneliness, sometimes disturbance of mind, sometimes lowness of heart, disappointment, frustration. Often, very often I was on my knees, but I never wanted to give up.'

'Sometimes those dark times lasted for minutes, sometimes hours, sometimes a few days. Throughout those ten years I was tempted during times like that, but I knew I was driven by the Holy Spirit to do it.'

'God spoke to me through all those days. I felt the power of His voice in my soul. When I was facing a trial, I prayed that He would make clear the reason for that trial, and once I heard clear words, "Don't be afraid, I am with you!" It was a time of great trials, but also great joy.'

And what, I asked, had been the fruit of those ten years? 'The grace of God', he replied. And did it live with him still? 'Of course!' he said. 'Sometimes here in the monastery I feel the Holy Spirit come down upon me and I want to shout to God in joy and gratitude.'

'When that happens, I close the door and windows of my cell because I am afraid that I am being too noisy for my neighbours. Once, a dove came to my window and started singing, and I just hoped that its voice was louder than mine.'

Mercurius took me to meet a second hermit, Father Azarias, who had been an officer in the Egyptian Army and fought in the wars of 1967 and 1973 before becoming a monk. When I met him, Azarias had been a hermit for 20 years. 'I am here', he said, 'in order to be closer to God on behalf of the whole of mankind – and to pray for the Islamic world also.'

He was living in great simplicity in a cave in the sand dunes. He sleeps on a bed of concrete, softened only by sheets of cardboard, but none the less has 'very deep and serene sleeps. I really feel that I am more comfortable and satisfied than the kings of this world.'

But, I said, he owned nothing. Azarias smiled, a gentle, beautiful smile. 'I own the heavens', he replied. Father Matta, who had first given him leave to become a hermit after some years in the monastery and had kept a continual watch over him during his early days in the desert with face-to-face meetings and letters, had lived far more simply than he did when he himself was a hermit.

Father Matta and his companions, said Azarias, had lived on food brought to them every three months by camel drivers and had planted simple grasses to sustain them in the meantime. At St Macarius, he said, he had tomatoes and cucumbers and could cook things for himself. Life was much more comfortable for him than it had been for them.

He had known Father Matta since 1948, said Father Youhanna, one of the monastery's elders. Matta had lived as a hermit in the desert for 30 years before the Coptic Pope, who had himself been a hermit, asked him to help revive St Macarius. Father Youhanna has a large, gentle face and the kindest of eyes. He conveys a sense of great warmth and inner peace.

'Matta was very convinced about his kind of monasticism', he said. 'For him, being a monk meant no speech, having relations with people only as God showed him. Living only for Christ, putting all his senses, ambitions, feelings at the service of Jesus.'

He himself had lived for years alongside Father Matta in a very distant desert. For three of those years he had been in a cave far from his companions. That had been the best time of all. What was so wonderful was the complete silence, no electricity, no modern devices. Even the water came from a spring in the ground. It made you feel very near to Jesus.

'In the beginning', said Youhanna, 'it was very difficult for me. I was a pharmacist and I'd come from the city where all my material needs were easily met. Suddenly I found myself sleeping on the ground! Yet, in the end, I felt those material needs were coming to me from heaven.'

'In all this, the silence is very important, because, in it, you can hear God. We live in a time when people are so busy and they find it good to spend all their time in busyness because that helps them to escape from themselves.'

If that was going to change, he said, they would have to reconsider their attitude to time, and then there would be a kind of giving and taking. If they gave time to silence and prayer, then – if his experience was anything to go by – they would be given eternity in return.

None of the monks I met at St Macarius spoke a single word about religious doctrine. It was always silence, silence, silence as the way to God. Even religious people, said one monk, thought of prayer as if it were a matter of speaking all the time, thereby making themselves God. Prayer was not intended to be a monologue, we were meant to be silent and listen for God's answers in our hearts.

One afternoon, I walked up through the dunes and sat by the grave of Father Matta, who died in 2006, and thought how strange it was that these men who have given up all the pleasures and possessions of this world should seem to be so full of joy, should have such clear, unlined faces, when those who drink deeply of those pleasures often look careworn and even ravaged.

The monks I had met, by denying themselves those pleasures and subjecting themselves to the rigours of life in the desert, had managed, as it seemed to me, to strip away the layers of drivenness, self-importance and indulgence, the heavy-duty clothing of self, with which the world encrusts so many of us, and now display a radiance which is unmistakeable. I would be only too happy to brave the mosquitoes and the food to share their life again.

For whatever reason, the monasteries and nunneries in the deserts of Egypt are flourishing. From St Macarius, I went to St Bishoy, where there are no less than 175 monks, many of whom were once doctors and engineers. One of the engineers played a considerable part in building a great new cathedral there some ten years ago.

It is the same at what is probably the oldest monastery in the world, St Anthony the Great, which stands at the foot of the South Galala mountains in Egypt's Eastern Desert. There are 120 monks and five more join the community every year.

St Anthony, who had been living closer to the River Nile, came to that place around the year 330 and stayed for 70 years. He lived in a cave about 1,000 feet up the mountain above where the monastery now stands and, according to Father Ruweis, my guide, occasionally came down to spend time with the other monks.

You have to climb 1,200 steps to reach the cave. It is a formidable undertaking. I was lucky to be climbing alone, in peace and total silence. It is as close as you can come, I would have thought, to what is often called the silence of eternity. As you climb, you see far below the great empty sweep of the Eastern Desert.

Eventually, at the top of the steps, you reach a large flat space and, beyond it, a sheer rock face with a cleft in it. There are some rather battered carpets at the entrance to what was once the cave in which St Anthony spent so many years. I squeezed myself along the cleft, went down some steps and found myself in a small room with a table and pictures of Christ and St Anthony. The monks regularly celebrate Mass here. It is a stark and lonely place.

Back in the monastery, I met Father Zosema, who is in his forties and was once an art director with Egyptian TV. He told me of the only time when he felt that he had heard God's voice. He spoke with great emotion, almost weeping, struggling to get the words out.

'I was in a lot of trouble just a year ago', he said. 'I felt I was going to collapse mentally. When I took on this life, God promised that he would be with me, that I would never feel alone – and yet I felt that I *was* alone. I asked why, and I struggled to get closer to God but felt no response from Him. In my distress I went up the mountain as you have just done.'

'Then I heard it and it was a voice. It simply said "I promised!" I turned round to look where it came from. Did it come from the left or the right, from above or below? I wondered if I had just imagined it but it was very clear and, after I had heard it, I felt a great sense of peace. That is a voice which you can only receive when you are in silence.'

For some reason – partly, no doubt, because I have a short fuse – this curious remark infuriated me. It also scored a bullseye on what, though I had never put it into words, was my central motive in life, a desire to climb the ladder of success.

What, I demanded to know, was unnatural about ambition? Even more infuriatingly, Jim just laughed and would say no more.

Then, a couple of months later, while we were having a cup of coffee after dinner in his room, he casually let me know in so many words that he thought me the most self-centred person he had ever met. This time, my reaction was more violent. I grabbed a piece of soap from his washbasin and threw it at him. He did not seem at all put out. He was a disturbing sort of fellow. You never knew what he might say next.

So much for the background to the evening that was to prove so momentous for me and that took place just a few weeks later. The setting was the same. Again, we were having a cup of coffee in Jim's quarters. Quite suddenly, and without any preliminaries, he asked whether I would like, as he put it, to 'listen to God'. If I had not been so stunned, I might have burst out laughing.

I knew that there existed ardent evangelicals who were apt to ask, sometimes in the most unsuitable circumstances, whether you were 'saved'. Indeed, there had been one such at Christ Church in Oxford, a gleaming-eyed man whose appearance in Tom Quad always sent me scampering off in the opposite direction. I had not expected to be trapped like this, on an occasion when I was hoping for nothing more than a friendly chat.

In any event, I thought it a preposterous suggestion. 'But', I said, 'I don't believe in God.' That did not faze Jim. My belief or lack of it

16

The power in silence

I still do not fully understand what happened that evening in Singapore so long ago. I mention it now only because it is, in large part, the reason why I decided to write this book. At the end of that evening, I was in no doubt about the power of silence.

It was a bizarre occasion and wholly unexpected, but it changed the course of my life. I was doing my National Service in the Royal Air Force – 'Bring a lounge suit and golf clubs', said the letter summoning me for officer training – and had been sent afterwards, at my own request, to Singapore in 1955. I wanted an adventure: far better, I felt, than 18 months eating egg and chips in somewhere like Bodmin.

Once there, I was befriended by a man who, like myself, came from the North of England and, like myself, worked in the education section on the RAF base at Changi.

Jim was cheerful and outspokenly Christian but, as our friendship developed, showed a propensity for being extremely irritating. One day, sitting together in the office, he asked me what I hoped to do when I went back to Britain. I replied that I had always wanted to work for what was then the *Manchester Guardian*. 'Oh,' said Jim, 'so you think personal ambition is a good thing.'

did not change God's position in the slightest, he replied. Thoroughly embarrassed as I was, I took that to be one of those glib responses that practised evangelicals produce to keep their targets on the hop. None the less it left me on the back foot, not knowing what to say next.

Jim's *coup de foudre* landed on what might have been thought rather infertile ground. True, I had been packed off to Sunday School and chapel, often three times on a Sunday, by parents who doubtless wanted relief from the demands of a hyperactive only child. True, I had later sung in the choir of the local Anglican Church, where I had exhibited a penchant for fainting at crucial moments in the services.

Even so, all that had left me with no interest whatsoever in religion. I had neither any conscious belief nor, for that matter, disbelief. So far as I was concerned, religion was a peripheral matter. What really interested me was winning cricket matches – I was the local Air Force captain – and musing about what I would do when I went back to Britain.

On the other hand, it is fair to say that although I had made a few superficially impressive steps up the ladder of success – a decent Oxford degree, a scholarship to the United States – there was within me a vague sense of unease, a feeling of not being entirely comfortable with myself and my life. My patina of self-confidence was thinner than it might have appeared.

Maybe that was why I did not bat away Jim's mention of God with a 'not on your life', or 'you cannot be serious'. Anyway, for whatever reason, I did not. My silence, my appearance of mute acquiescence, was quite enough to give him the go-ahead.

'Why don't we be quiet?' he said. 'Just think of the uncompromising standards of Jesus Christ's life and teaching and see whether God says anything to you.' He gave me a pencil and a piece of paper so that I could jot down any thoughts that came to me. So, like a sheep dumb before its shearer, I just sat there and waited.

I expected nothing. It had never once, in my 20-odd years, occurred to me that being silent might be a useful activity. In fact, I had never thought about it as a concept. If I had, I am sure I would have reckoned it a boring, pointless way to waste one's time when there were always so many interesting things to do.

In the event, I did not have long to wait. Almost immediately, a thought flashed into my mind. It was, in fact, rather more than a thought. It almost sounded as if it were spoken by someone else inside me, and in a rather peremptory way. 'You are a dictator on the cricket field', came the words. 'Apologise to your team!'

I was astonished. I had never consciously had any thought of that kind, indeed I had never thought about my behaviour on the cricket field at all. All I had ever thought about was winning. Yet it rang true. I was the only officer in the team and, although not unduly lofty, I did tend to give orders to the other ranks, who included three talented Australians.

At that moment, hearing those words, I had a sense that there was something, somewhere out there, that knew me better than I knew myself. Because of the way I had been brought up and all those years in Sunday School, I instinctively labelled that something God.

Other thoughts followed, and all of them had something of the same imperious quality as the first. 'When you went up to Oxford,' came the next thought, 'you became a snob. Write and apologise to your parents.'

Again, I had not had any such thought before, but I knew what it meant. My father, who by this time was a school caretaker, had the extraordinary knack of eating quite large numbers of peas using only a knife and I had fancied that that sort of thing would not go down too well at Christ Church. As a result, I had never invited my parents to Oxford.

Then there were three boys whom I had treated badly at school. Again, more letters, more apologies. Girls I had mistreated … it went on and on – and always, with each thought, what I ought to do.

Thinking about it now, it does rather sound as if, before that evening with Jim, I had been riven by a huge sense of guilt and that the flood burst when he cornered me. Memory, of course, can play strange tricks on all of us, but so far as I can recall I did not suffer – if that is the right word – from any sense of guilt and I was certainly not, as the saying goes, 'looking for something'. All of which makes it more difficult to account for what happened.

Oddly enough, when I told the story to people I met while gathering material for this book, nobody said that they regarded the whole thing as a complete delusion on my part. Perhaps they were just being polite. In any event, it invariably deepened the discussion.

The Hindus and Christians tended to think that God had had some part, probably a considerable one, in it all. My Zen Buddhist friend Mike reckoned that, because of the shock Jim's bizarre invitation had given me, I had suddenly been put in touch with what was already there waiting in the intuitive, right side of my brain.

Other Buddhists maintained that I had always known that my behaviour was ripe for amendment and that the occasion had simply unlocked that knowledge. 'You realised you were a jerk on the cricket field,' said Amaro Bhikku, the abbot of the Amaravati monastery, 'but it was all buried under the life of conditioning you had had. You wanted to win, to look good, and your intuitive wisdom never got to the surface because of your desire for success and your wish to impress others.'

I understood what they were all saying and no doubt there was a great deal of truth in much of it, but I still did not find these explanations wholly satisfactory. For one thing, as I say, I had not had any heart-searchings about the areas to which the thoughts drew my attention so forcibly. More to the point, the thoughts that popped into my mind really did seem to come from elsewhere.

It was as if someone or something was speaking to me. Nor did the thoughts convey a vague sense that I needed to do something about my life. They had a decisive and unequivocal quality that could hardly have sprung from some general sense of dissatisfaction. Could it have had some connection with what Christians call God?

Taken together, the thoughts that came to me amounted to the beginning of a programme for a new way of life. Given my disinterest in religion, I do not think I could possibly have concocted them for myself.

Were I to claim, in today's world, that God had spoken to me, I would be written off as delusional if not actually mentally deranged. So perhaps it is better to call the thoughts interior locutions and leave it at that.

Yet, having begun that time in silence as, at best, an agnostic, I came out of it as some sort of believer, at least to the extent that it never occurred to me not to obey what I had been told to do. And, for some reason that again I cannot adequately explain, I left that room walking on air, not on account of some so-called achievement but because I felt a sense of release, of freedom and a quite new kind of happiness inside.

What is more, having found that a time spent in silence could be infinitely more fruitful than I had ever bargained for, I was eager to repeat the dose, alone, early the next morning.

In the following days, I did everything I had been told to do: letters, apologies, all to the best of my ability. The cricket team got quite a shock, but soon recovered. From then on, I made a practise of spending time in silence in the early morning. What came to me over the years in those times played a decisive part in my choice of career and whom I asked to marry me.

With all my flaws and foolhardiness, silence has always been an unfailing guide and companion. In a way, this book is my thank you to silence.

That is quite enough about me – or almost enough. Given the nature of my experience, I was particularly interested in whether other people had had these so-called interior locutions, and how it had affected their lives. It is not that I regard such experiences as a sign of divine favour – I know many profoundly religious people who have never had one – but they do nevertheless intrigue me.

What has struck me about those who claim to have had them is how very rare they seem to be, even in lives totally devoted to serving their god. For example, I had expected monks and nuns to have had any number of these experiences, for them to be almost routine events in their lives, given that they are supposed to be 'closer to God' than the rest of us.

I had even wondered whether the less scrupulous among them might lay claim to having heard 'voices' on a number of occasions just to indicate that they were on particularly close terms with the Almighty! I was surprised to discover that the opposite is often the case.

I spoke with, among others, three nuns, one Catholic and two Anglican, all of whom had been in their orders for decades. Yet each of them had had only one experience that she was prepared to describe as an interior locution and, in one instance, it had happened long before she became a nun.

'I personally have known God speak in a word only once', said Sister Mary of St Joseph, who is the prioress of the Carmelite convent at Ladbroke Grove in London. 'I was eight or nine at the time and, during a week of special devotion, our priest said that we should ask God what we could do to really please Him. If we asked, he said, we would receive an answer.'

'I remember being quite intrigued by that, so, kneeling along with my sisters before the Blessed Sacrament, I asked God what He wanted of me. The answer came almost before I was ready. It was just the word "Pray!" The word uttered itself, I didn't hear it with my ears but it didn't come from anywhere within me.'

'I thought it was a funny answer and a rather dull one. I thought "I do that already," and forgot about it. I had expected something like "help your mother" or "help your sisters." What's more, when I became a Carmelite nun, I made no mental connection between having heard that instruction and what I'd decided to give my life to.

The remarkable thing to me is that that word fulfilled itself without any intention on my part.'

So far as I can see, there is no knowing when or why these locutions take place, though they often seem to occur at what might be called crossroads moments in people's lives.

'In my early thirties', said Miles, a Scotsman from Glasgow who reckoned to spend time regularly in silent devotion, 'I was working for a company in Wiltshire. Having just turned 30, I felt the time might have come to consider marriage. A girl from one of the families in our social group attracted me and I sensed a possible reciprocal feeling in her. The idea, however, had got no further than conjecture.'

'Then one day, returning to my place of work after a weekend visit to my parents, I was sitting in a train compartment at Paddington on a cold winter evening. Should I, I began wondering, advance this idea of a closer relationship with the girl I had in mind. On one of the very few occasions when it seemed to me that there was someone else there talking to me, I heard the devastating sentence, "You are always free to choose second best." '

'In an instant, I knew that she was not the person I was meant to marry. It was eight years later that the right person was given to me.'

So much for interior locutions, which arrive in a form that is akin to the spoken word. Others who do not claim to have ever heard any kind of 'voice' have none the less had experiences of unexpected, irritatingly persistent thoughts which, because they paid heed to them, spared them (and others) from disaster or at least grave risk.

Jagdish Joshi is a Hindu Brahmin who, as a young man, made a practise of sitting in silence for a few minutes each day to address his routine priorities. In 1972 he started work as a site supervisor for a construction company. They were building a large well for a village in a remote area. The excavation of the soil was almost complete and they were hurrying to build the well's retaining walls before the monsoon arrived.

One evening, after sunset, when work had stopped for the day, Joshi was taking a stroll along the bank above a dried-up riverbed when he had the persistent thought that they should *immediately* move the site of the labourers' camp to a higher location.

He resisted the idea for some considerable time. The labourers, of whom there were 115, were after all utterly exhausted at the end of a long, hot day. The thought, however, simply refused to go away, so he gathered the labourers' leaders together and told them that, even though it was pitch dark, they were going to move their camp to a different location.

They were naturally reluctant to go along with the idea, but Joshi insisted and ordered extra lanterns to be brought from the village. They spent the next three or four hours moving the camp to higher ground.

Early the next morning there was a loud noise and, for a few moments, the earth shook. At first light, Joshi found to his horror that the land near the excavation site had slid away and the place where the labourers' camp had been was now a huge hole.

He had had, he told me, a not dissimilar experience while he was taking a group of teenagers round northern India as part of a Rotary International Students' Exchange programme. One evening, after they had finished sightseeing and were driving back to their hotel, the local guide suggested that they should all go out again after dinner to a night bazaar so that their foreign visitors could have a 'bargain shopping experience'.

Everyone liked the idea but, while Joshi was taking a shower, he had a strong and persistent thought that he should call off the outing and organise a talent show on the hotel's lawns instead. Next morning, while he was settling the hotel bill, he heard the people at the desk talking about the night bazaar where they had been planning to spend the previous evening.

There had apparently been communal violence, and a lot of damage had been done to both vehicles and property. A mob had looted the shops and attacked tourists. Joshi draws the conclusion, from this and other experiences, that it is a good idea to heed one's inner voice.

Some rather surprising people have turned to silence for help, particularly in moments of great need, but for some reason have preferred to say nothing about it. Winston Churchill was one such.

Dr Josephine Butler worked closely with the Prime Minister during the Second World War and afterwards wrote about her experiences in her book *Churchill's Secret Agent*.

In it, she recalls a surprising exchange with the Prime Minister. She had been present at a meeting during which Churchill had said that he wanted to replace the general in charge of operations in Africa. Almost all the War Cabinet were against the man he had in mind. 'I said that, when I was troubled, I had always prayed and meditated and it brought results. I knew that he too meditated. He turned to me in surprise and said "you are very observant. Most people imagine I just catnap."' (*Churchill's Secret Agent*, Exeter: Blaketon-Hall, 1983; p. 36.)

Jonathan Sacks, Britain's outstanding Chief Rabbi, is another who, thus far, has preferred to say nothing about his practise of silence. 'We're not very much into silence in Judaism,' he said with an ironic smile, 'but I do spend a lot of time listening to God, in silence.'

Sacks turned to the female assistant who was sitting with us. 'How long have you known me?' he asked. 'Forty-three years', she replied. 'And have I ever spoken of this before?' he asked. She shook her head.

This, said Sacks, was indeed the first time he had ever spoken of it. There had been a sect of Jewish mystics, the Hasidim, who had made a discipline of silence, and he did the same thing.

'In silence', he went on, 'you can hear something that is not just a product of your own personality, something that stands outside and says "this is where you need to be'. It tells me when I'm doing something wrong and what I should do to put it right, and, when I'm doing something right, that I should stick with it.'

'I don't regard it as infallible, and it doesn't translate itself into words but into feelings and, sometimes, a call to do something.' Others, he added, might call it intuition. For him, though, there was more to it than that.

'There is in the Bible', he said, 'the famous story of Elijah the prophet. Jezebel wants his blood and he goes to Mount Horeb. There he hears what I think is best translated as "a slender silence" (the King James Bible renders it as "a still, small voice').'

'Now that is a sound that you can only hear if you are listening, and that is the way God speaks in silence. We have to create a silence in the soul so that we can hear Him listening to us and speaking in a faint way.'

I asked Sacks to unpack for me the famous Hasidic saying that 'the altar dearest to God is the altar of silence'.

'The most famous line in Jewish prayer', he replied, 'is "Hear O Israel, the Lord our God is one." In my own translation I rendered that as "Listen O Israel," because I wanted people to understand that hearing God is a very active form of listening, it is not passive. When Moses says that, he's commanding his people to listen to God.'

'I don't regard any of what comes to me in silence as being in the category of revelation,' Sacks went on, 'but I do spend a lot of time in silence and, in that silence, I discover what I need to do, say, how I need to lead.'

'Modern life does not give us enough time for silence. We have to listen to hear the music beneath the noise. That's what I think religious faith is about, the ability to hear the music beneath the noise.'

Richard Chartres, the Anglican Bishop of London, fully shares Sacks's reverence for silence. 'Every morning when I've read the Scriptures for the day and said my prayers, I spend half an hour in wordless prayer, reaching beyond, being tolerant of things as they come up. If something clamorous arises, I just note it and move on. As the Kipling poem says, to treat those two impostors just the same, not to be elated by triumph or depressed by disaster.'

'I don't hear voices, but I do receive communications from God. There is the light which reveals with awful clarity the parts of my life which are exposed as unauthentic, and then being shown what has to be done about them.'

'It is guidance, but it doesn't come in sentences. In your daily listening, like me, you will meet angels, messengers of God, either then or during the course of the day. Some other person will speak words which have an extra specific gravity, words of power. You should receive those words not as pieces of information, but as messages coming from God.'

Chartres's sort of Christian seems to be someone who aspires to be a constant listener. 'If you begin to enter that darkness, to engage in profound listening, you can hear those messages from angels every day. The spiritual life means waking up, it is the capacity to watch and listen. That is how we are meant to live, so that things reverberate in our inner spaces and don't just bounce off the surface.'

For Chartres, putting our feet on that road, trying to become that sort of person, involves breaking through the crust which all of us construct to protect us from the perils, pressures and disappointments of this life, the slings and arrows of outrageous fortune, better known as Murphy's Law. Until that crust is broken, he says, 'we are like ailing fish trapped beneath it.' Such a breakthrough, he adds, requires silence and stillness, which – for him – are 'the great educators, because they deflect the pressures of the passing moment.'

'As we break through that crust, we enter what I would call the psychic zone where there are great shadows, great fears, cravings, lusts, where you are shown what you don't like about yourself and all the things you have covered up over the years.'

'One of the laws of the spiritual life is that what you cover up has the power to damage you profoundly. If, on the other hand, you can face those things, you can take away their power to do you irremediable harm. And then, assisted by a guide, like Virgil escorting Dante through the Inferno, you can find your way to a new and different life.'

What was vital in navigating through the psychic zone, he went on, was that we should plunge ourselves into silence. That could, in some ways, be like 'a foretaste of death', as we encountered all the shadows and terrors, but if there was a real letting go of the crust, of our old life, then we would be greeted and upheld.

'If we can commit ourselves to exploring those inner spaces with real integrity, then we will be surprised by joy – a joy which will not fade away because it comes from an inexhaustible fountain beyond ourselves. And we will discover that silence is the most speaking thing in the world.

'We must, though, be absolutely scrupulous in all this not to seek to cultivate those interior states which we find agreeable. People may be looking for peace and a sense of inner calm, and those are not ignoble ambitions, but they can also be the enemies of progress – so that we never arrive at the place where we say "now I know nothing," where we encounter a mystery.'

'That is not a puzzle that can be sorted out by some Hercule Poirot with his little grey cells, but it is a mystery that includes you. There is no fathoming of that mystery. It is imponderable. As St Paul says, "in Him we live and move and have our being."'

If Chartres is right, steeping oneself in silence and abiding by its insights is not something to be undertaken lightly or ill-advisedly. As he portrays it, it sounds like an interesting adventure for those with the stomach for it, but not necessarily a comfortable one.

What writing this book has shown me is that silence has immense power, in all kinds of ways. It is a vital ingredient in both music and drama. It is the cradle of creativity, the mental space in which all great art has been conceived. It is an invaluable tool for both the psychotherapist and the priest.

It can be freely drawn upon by those who seek God or enlightenment in the search for self-understanding, self-mastery or self-healing. At a more modest level, it can give us a blessed respite from the clamour of everyday life.

Yet for most people in the West it remains a zero, a nothing, a blank space, the very fount of boredom – and, very often, a malign and miserable space as well. It can deepen a sense of loneliness, heighten a feeling of regret or guilt, allow hates and hurts to fester.

We at least have the free will to choose what it will be for us. It is at our beck and call, ours to command: an enemy from which we flee, or an ever-present, ever-courteous friend. If we choose to treat it as a friend, it can give us all manner of things: a way to order our lives, insight into ourselves and others and, for the religious believer, a means of tapping into a wisdom far greater than our own.

I salute all those, from any and every walk of life, who recognise the value of silence and have been trained to use it with the skill and discretion that it demands and deserves. And to those who have never tried to tap its riches, I would say: give it a try, there is nothing to be lost. There may be no quick pay-off but, if you ignore its possibilities, you may be robbing yourself of a great and enriching adventure in travelling through what is, after all, our own, unique inner universe.

INDEX